1. If you are a "silent sufferer", what can you learn about your disorder to help your own situation?

2. If you are a family member or friend of a "silent sufferer", what knowledge will help you and help them?

3. If you are a primary care doctor or other health professional medical prescriber, what can you do to help your existing patients?

4. If you are a health care system leader, can you help by seeing that screening, brief intervention and referral to treatment as well as expanded patient support and monitoring after treatment becomes an integral part of your care network?

5. If you are a government leader or public official, can you insure public policies and programs to promote better quality care through stronger oversight, regulation and performance metrics of treatment providers?

Book Design & Production:
Columbus Publishing Lab
www.ColumbusPublishingLab.com

Copyright © 2025 by Greg Wince

All rights reserved.
This book, or parts thereof, may not be
reproduced in any form without permission.

Hardback ISBN: 978-1-63337-896-4
Paperback ISBN: 978-1-63337-895-7
Ebook ISBN: 978-1-63337-897-1

Printed in the United States of America
1 3 5 7 9 10 8 6 4 2

COACH'S STORY AND HANDBOOK
VOLUME I

SUBSTANCE ADDICTION AND "THE SILENT SUFFERERS"

GREG WINCE
WITH RICHARD WHITNEY, M.D.

THIS BOOK IS WRITTEN FOR

Over ten years ago, I began to write this book for my children and grandchildren. I wanted to educate them regarding the nature of my alcohol use disease. I realized that the genetic component is a primary risk factor for the disease.

I had no plans to publish until last year when I was encouraged to share my story and the knowledge I have gathered over the years. For several decades, with the exceptional guidance of Dr. Richard Whitney, I have studied what happened to me and why. This is my experience.

This series of handbooks, in addition to my own family, is being written for the:

1. **"Silent Sufferers"** who have or are currently being tormented by alcohol and other (legal and illegal) substance misuse and use disorders
2. **Families and close associates of "Silent Sufferers",** who have experienced ongoing, related, negative and costly consequences
3. **Communities, schools, employers and business** personnel being challenged beyond reasonable limits by increasing alcohol and drug use
4. **The General Public,** who largely do not understand or don't yet mentally accept the chronic, progressive, modern medical disease model of alcohol and other substance use disorders, yet pay a price of billions of dollars in financial costs, lives and lost productivity (with a currently failing, "siloed" system of unregulated addiction care operating outside the mainstream medical system).
5. **Medical Doctors and Prescribing Professionals** in existing mainstream practices, who for a variety of reasons, are not utilizing the basic Screening, Brief Intervention and Referral to Treatment (SBIRT) method nor providing proven medical-assisted treatment (MAT) for the top treatable public health disease in our nation.
6. **Public Health System and Health Insurance Company Executives,** who with cooperatively improved corporate strategic planning using performance metrics and value-added principles could develop a much more navigable and less financially wasteful addiction care infrastructure expanding far more patient outreach, availability, accessibility, screening and earlier assessment.
7. **Government Leaders and Public Officials** who have the responsibility to:

- Ensure adequate public resources are provided to address the broad scope of substance related issues facing our society and communities
- Establish statewide delivery systems of quality addiction care geographically available and accessible to all residents
- Involve mainstream medical practices as key entry points for substance use and mental health screening, brief intervention and referral to treatment
- Establish firm operational and clinical standards, regulations and monitoring of all assessment/treatment facilities to ensure quality care
- Create and utilize specialized and standardized methods of provider performance data collection with public information transparency

"Recovery is driven by the pursuit of meaning and purpose." Gabor Maté, M.D.[1]

"More, Broader, Kinder, Earlier, Faster, Better, Longer!"

DEDICATION

This book is dedicated to Beverly Ann Wince, my beautiful, loving and talented wife, a wonderful mother, devoted grandmother, outstanding teacher and great friend with whom I have been married to for 57 years and who just passed on in May, 2024.

Bev has been my rock, a steady foundation for me and our family in our ups and downs with my alcohol use disorder. She taught me so much about unselfish love, compassion, commitment and the courage to change. To the end of her days on earth, she adored our children and grandchildren. She continuously cultivated her close "sister" friendships, her interest in spiritual matters and her love of nature; continually demonstrating an enduring strength, a curiosity for learning and a special dignity. In her last days fighting cancer, she still continued to enthusiastically encourage me to finish this book. Here is to you, my love.

I am yours
the way the sea
belongs to the moon
belongs to the sky,
and even if the jealous stars
break and shatter
upon the Milky Way
I will still see heaven in your eyes
—Mark Anthony

TABLE OF CONTENTS

PRE-SEASON PREPARATION — 9

Introduction — 11
The Opening Tip: Jump Ball Quiz — 13
Why Me, Why Write This Book — 15
What Is Driving The Addiction Epidemic Of Legal And Illegal Substances — 17
Social Impact — 18
A Glimpse of The Opponent — 22
The Fundamentals of Addiction Physiology — 23
Who Are We Failing Today? — 24
A Direct Challenge To Mainstream Medical Practice Doctors — 24
For Public and Private Insurance Payers — 25

THE GAME: COACH'S STORY — 27

1945: Genetic Predisposition — 29
My Turn: Childhood Trauma and the Age of Onset — 32
Experimental/Recreational Use — 34
The Binge/Intoxication Stage — 34
The Withdrawal/Negative Affect Stage — 43
Torn in Half/Feeling Like "Yuk" — 46
The Anger Monster — 46
The Preoccupation/Anticipation Stage — 48
The Basement Floor — 50
The Terms of Surrender — 52
The Gift of Recovery Accepted — 53

SCOUTING THE OPPONENT: ALCOHOL AND OTHER SUBSTANCE USE DISORDERS — 57

"Modern Medical Disease Model" of Substance Use Disorder (SUD) — 59
A Basic Pattern of All Mind-Altering Substances in The Brain — 60
US Drinking Characteristics — 61
The Treadmill, the Silent Assassins, and the Sledgehammer — 61

"Using Responsibly" Not the Norm	63
A Path to Dysfunction	63
The Known Causes and Stages of Substance Use Diseases	64
The Opponent: Fundamentals	70
The Opponent: Strategies And Processes	76
The Reason I Drank	79
The Process of Becoming Addicted to Alcohol	79
Physiological Differences of Individuals with Alcohol Use Disorder (AUD)	80
The Three Cyclical Stages of Substance Addiction	82
Tolerance in Addiction	83
Withdrawal (Abstinence Syndrome) of Substance Addiction	84
Capture and Craving	85
Physical Consequences of Extended Alcohol Use	87
Physical Consequences of Other Drug Use	88
Social and Emotional Consequences of Alcohol/Drug Use	88
Spiritual Consequences of Addiction	88
The Opponent: The Full Court Press	89
Cues in Addiction	92
Addictive Behavior	94
The Opponent: The Disconnects of the Addicted Person	97
Natural Human Goals vs. Addicted Person Goals	98
Effects of Substance Use on Learning, Memory, and Motivation	99
Stress and Alcohol: The Double Whammy	102
Drugs and the Brain in Substance Addiction	103
The Fundamentals of Mind-Altering Drugs	104
Opponent Process Theory	105
Alcohol Hangovers, Blackouts, and Poisoning	105

GAMETIME ADJUSTMENTS: THE CURRENT STATE OF SUBSTANCE USE DISORDER TREATMENT AND RECOVERY   109

Substance Addiction is a Primary, Chronic, Progressive Disease	111
Public Health Disease Number One	111

Our Alcohol Driven Culture	113
The Public Bias: "Good Drugs" and "Bad Drugs"	115
US Culture and Alcohol Intrinsically Woven Together	115
Harm Reduction and the Myth of "Controlled Drinking"	115
Addiction Care Problems in the Current Public Health System	116
The Merry-Go-Round In The Wild West Of "Rehab"	118
Caution About the Quality of Recovery Treatment, Unproven Ideas and Undocumented Programs	120
Behavioral Counseling Not the Best Starting Place for Treatment of a Substance Use Disorder (SUD)	121
Words Matter!	121
The Modern Medical Disease Model of Treatment for Patients and Families	122
An Example of a Quality Care Treatment Facility	122
Gratitude for Miracles	124
Recovery Requirement: Daily Fundamental Practice	125
A Team of Champions	125
The Rooms of Shock and Awe	127
"Half-Measures Availed Us Nothing"	128
"Don't Think"	128
Ask The Team Doc	131
Do Our Current Policies Contribute to Relapse?	136
Myths and Facts	139

THE OPPONENT: A LOADED ROSTER — 145

The Opponent's Roster	147
Basic Lineup of Addictive Drugs	147
The Opponent Roster: Alcohol	147
Recent Research: Alcohol	148
Other Basic Types of Drugs	155

POSTGAME ANALYSIS: APPENDICES AND REFERENCES — 167

Acknowledgements	169
About the (Coach) Author	171

TABLE OF CONTENTS

About the Team Doc	173
Coming Soon	175
Recommended Reads About Substance Use Disorders	177
Endnotes	181

PRE-SEASON PREPARATION

INTRODUCTION

The Coach's Handbook

In this Coach's Handbook Series (Volume I), we present an overview of substance addictions or what the medical community defines as "a disease spectrum" or continuum of Substance Use Disorders. Our intention is to provide information that will assist the vast numbers of individuals and families suffering silently from the use of legal drugs, in addition to illicit substances that are easily available in our country. Another goal is to help reduce the alarming rates of relapse of people identified with the disease who have experienced some level of addiction treatment or counseling. Our focus is primarily on alcohol and other legal drugs.

Our call for systemic change begins by identifying: (a) the glaring absence of a majority of mainstream medical practitioners who need to be screening and initially intervening with chronic addiction disease identification; (b) the present poor quality of most treatment centers as unregulated "rehabs," and (c) the absence of sufficient patient aftercare, support and chronic care monitoring after intervention and treatment occurs. With few other chronic diseases do we ignore initial screening or chronic care management.

Major changes are needed to the mainstream public health care system, health insurance practices/processes and a more supportive governmental approach to normalizing and regulating the quality standards of addiction disease care. We are advocates for a significant increase in the quality of assessment and treatment facilities. Quality should be regulated closely and should have to meet stringent medical standards of care and performance criteria prior to receiving public or private fees.

Our concept of systemic change is supported by proven, evidence-based strategies, and operational or clinical best practices combined with innovative approaches. The broader, long-term aim of our proposed change is to shift the paradigm of the public perspective of this devastating, chronic medical disease, and to expedite the earlier availability, easier accessibility and affordability of quality treatment for substance misuse and disorders in this country. We, as a society, deserve better.

In Coach's Handbook Volume II, which is planned for release later this year, we detail what we have actually experienced to be a successful, comprehensive, modern medical model of recovery, administered based upon individual needs in a quality treatment environment. In Volume II, a practical approach to spirituality will be offered. By encouraging an individual spiritual journey or path, we emphasize restoring relationships/connections in recovery, utilizing a "Higher Power" concept that anyone can accept, regardless of background, belief or a lack thereof.

Perhaps most importantly, in both Volumes I and II, we point out in detail the current obstacles to sufficient quality and reasonable costs for addiction care in the United States. Our Vision of Hope begins here.

THE OPENING TIP: JUMP BALL QUIZ

Note: Jot down your answers before you read this book, then scan it later. Grade yourself on the questions before and after you read this handbook.

1. Which drugs are a threat to your health? To your life? To others?

2. Which substances are more damaging in lives, financial loss, family dysfunction, premature diseases and deaths?

3. Which drugs are legal and illegal, and which are easier to access today?

4. What are the leading causes of preventable deaths in the United States?

5. Why is it so difficult for someone with an alcohol and/or drug problem to admit it?

6. How often are you screened by your family doctor for alcohol or any other substance use?

7. Why is it so difficult for someone seeking help to find the quality of care they need?

8. Why do most people who do find treatment find themselves drinking or using again within 12 months?

9. I introduce myself as having an alcohol use disorder, not an alcoholic. Why?

10. My brother, from the same biological parents, has no problem with alcohol. Why me?

11. Chemicals can be used for medical or recreational use. Which are for self-care and which are for getting high?

12. Are the cannabis products of today similar to the marijuana smoked twenty years ago?

WHY ME, WHY WRITE THIS BOOK

"MORE, BROADER, EARLIER, KINDER, FASTER, BETTER, LONGER"

Here's a staggering fact. Less than 5 percent of all individuals who have an alcohol or substance use disorder *ever* get any help, let alone initial quality medical or collaborative chronic care![2]

I am "Coach" Greg W., and I used to introduce myself as an *alcoholic* in my recovery groups. Now, using a more medically accurate, appropriate, and less stigmatizing label, I am a person with an *alcohol use disorder* (AUD). I am writing with the assistance of a highly respected and experienced professional, a doctor of addiction medicine and a doctor of psychology who specializes in child, family, and addiction psychology.

I am writing this series of "coaching" handbooks on *addiction, recovery*, and *a practical spirituality* that can help guide personal change. A *new vision of hope* is woven throughout the series to create earlier, more and better quality care through *a complete* system transformation. The key elements of transformational change we advocate are:

- Incorporating SBIRT (Screening, Brief Intervention and Referral to Treatment) into existing mainstream medical practices
- Providing longer chronic care support and monitoring after initial treatment
- Creating statewide addiction care delivery systems
- Establishing a statewide data system of composite patient activity and provider performance
- Building family/friend education into early patient care

A new system of addiction care requires provider and patient accountability with transparency in public reporting.

Currently our "siloed" system of unregulated, unmonitored, expensive and scattered "programs" and "rehabs" achieve dismal results. The extraordinary relapse rates experienced within one year after initial treatment are unacceptable. Only a very small percentage of people with alcohol or other substance misuse disorders ever get any help. Of those who do find their way to a facility, a considerable number are misdiagnosed and often receive only short term or inadequate care.

Unfortunately many health professionals in rehab programs are not addiction specialists or sufficiently trained in the modern medical disease model of addiction care. Addiction medical doctors, psychiatrists and psychologists are not trained the same way and have different perspectives and methods on how to treat addiction. I want a trained addiction medicine professional to treat me first for my specific and primary medical disease, unless I am first in need of emergency care for acute symptoms.

In this country we are in dire need of "more, broader, earlier, kinder, faster, better, longer" ways that folks with alcohol and other substance use disorders, especially from legal drug use, are identified, screened, assessed and receive collaborative care and continual support, monitoring and coaching with this chronic disease. There is no excuse for the enormous gap between the knowledge that has evolved in the scientific community to counter addiction and the actual "siloed", haphazard, unregulated, unmeasured practice of recovery that largely exists today.

Currently, this inadequately functioning "siloed system" of addiction care most often operates in its own vacuum, outside of the reach of mainstream medical practices and primary care professionals. The reasons for this essentially scattergun approach to substance addiction care are many.

The results are too clear! Over nine in ten people with a substance use disease never get help. Only one in ten people who are diagnosed receive any type of specialized medical treatment. And over half of all people diagnosed with a substance disorder relapse within the first year after initial treatment.[3] Sadly many current facilities promote themselves but lack the necessary staff and elements of quality addiction care and are, in reality, "relapse generators".

Systemic flaws in the public health system, many to do with stigmatization and a general lack of disease knowledge within the primary care medical system, have resulted in what I refer to as an ignored and forgotten but privately expanding group of "**silent sufferers**."

The key changes needed are to incorporate addiction screening, brief intervention and treatment into mainstream medical practices, providing longer chronic care support and monitoring, and establishing appropriate performance measurement and analytics.

This group of silent sufferers often gets ill and dies more slowly and secretly than the more publicized opioid or fentanyl-related addiction overdose deaths. Of course, most who die of illegal drugs begin as young people experimenting with legal mind-altering substances like alcohol and marijuana/cannabis products, in addition to tobacco products.

Individuals, regardless of age, when developing mild or moderate substance disorders, are rarely identified, especially early in their drinking or other drug misuse. Sometimes they just disappear. Little medical intervention occurs in the "misuse" stage of disease development. Neither individuals with this disease nor their families are adequately educated or screened early and often enough. Most silent sufferers reach a moderate to severe stage of their disease without obtaining the help that could prevent them and their families from experiencing many destructive consequences and premature deaths.

In 1976, nearly seven decades ago, the American Medical Association (AMA) officially designated substance addiction as an official medical disease.[4] Since then, technological advances, neurological research, the human genome discoveries, brain imaging, and the best practices of addiction care have developed and been demonstrated through extensive field trials. We have all the available knowledge we need to effectively deal with, but not cure, most chronic substance use disorders.

Yet our present mainstream medical system (our medical schools and especially family and internal medicine doctors, pediatricians, emergency physicians, et al.) are decades behind the science. There is still a general lack of training, knowledge, motivation, interest, and/or payer financial incentives to provide sufficient, quality disease care.

The result is that individuals in the formative years of a substance use disorder fail to self-identify or are not medically screened or identified in the early stages, when care and education have a chance to ward off further damage. Without intervention in a familiar setting visited regularly by patients, individuals develop their disease slowly, silently, steadily. Individuals with developing substance use disorders are often treated for organ damage and other side effects of their disease, but the primary disease itself is ignored.

A recent investigative study by a twelve-person team, "Physician Reluctance to Intervene in Addiction," published in July 2024 in JAMA Network Open,[5] identified the primary reasons physicians gave for not intervening in addiction. These responses of reluctance to treat were (1) the lack of institutional support (81.2%); (2) lack of skill (73.9%); cognitive capacity (73.5%); and knowledge (71.9%). Reimbursement concerns for time spent were also noted, as well as practice setting and drug type.

The researchers endorse targeting these reasons for reluctance expressed by physicians by requiring education and training, policy development, and clinical program implementation to remedy these barriers to effective substance use disorder care.

Unfortunately, the long-term, chronic disease management tools required to counter the relapsing nature of substance use disorders are unavailable to the vast majority of the general public.

Recent scientific gains and technological advances, such as brain imaging advances, now provide us with the sufficient medical knowledge we need to treat alcohol and most other substance use disorders. Likewise research has provided many proven clinical care best practices to significantly lower disease relapse rates.

Yet we continue to wastefully spend billions of dollars on the current failed "silo" system of unregulated, short-term addiction rehabs. Ironically, we don't use the term "rehab" when referring to patients with other chronic diseases. What we should do is provide early screening, intervention, and education with referrals to qualified specialists, and we continually encourage, support, and monitor the patient's progress and needs.

WHAT IS DRIVING THE ADDICTION EPIDEMIC OF LEGAL AND ILLEGAL SUBSTANCES

We know the reported overdose death rate of fentanyl-laced opiates has become an epidemic. We also know that overall identifiable substance addiction incidence and relapse rates, especially for young people, women, and seniors are increasing. What is often not factored into this incidence data are the unreported individuals suffering in secrecy, without visibility. I believe the rates of substance misuse are far greater than traditional surveys show.

Even non-substance addiction or behavioral addiction is rising in occurrence. This includes being addicted to eating, gambling, violence, gun use, technology use (internet, texting, smart phone, online purchasing, pornography, purchasing, body image, aggressive driving, ideas like conspiracy theories), and of course, the general eternal desires for possessions, pleasures, and power. All of these accelerating desires of contemporary society can have devastating consequences for people.

In his book *In the Realm of Hungry Ghosts*, Dr. Gabor Maté quotes Alice Miller describing addiction as "a flight from distress."[6] We all have desires that can obsessively become more than passions. With an alcohol use disorder, I was also addicted to work and achievement to feel better about myself.

Addiction is a human condition. In Buddhism, *dukkha* is a core belief in the idea that "life is suffering" and can result from the dissatisfaction with the typical circumstances of our human existence. Dukkha can result from our normal experiences of life, like birth, accidents, illness, and death; the constantly changing nature of life; and the impermanence of life itself.[7]

Dr. Maté refers to the human condition as a continuum, from consciousness at one end, and slavery and imprisonment on the opposite pole. He clarifies that "thinking" and "consciousness" are not the same, but that thinking is just a small part of consciousness.

Mass consumerism helps create and provoke our "want" to feel better. In the world today, it's easy to allow our "wanting" to flourish without consciousness. Often, we are relatively certain what we want will satisfy our emotional angst. Wanting internal peace from external sources doesn't work for long, and we try again to find some external pleasure or relief from stress. This cycle can lead from want to desire or passion to obsession without much consciousness.[8]

In his classic theological treatise, James Stalker described "wanting" as the cardinal or deadly sin of "appetite."[9] His "wanting" referred to anything we don't really need to survive or to experience safety and personal growth. The opposite of desire, according to the Hebrew word for "advent," means to "stop wanting, watch and wait for the next miracle to happen." Waiting is not our most prevalent social norm today.

Addiction is the manifestation of the paradox between wanting and our inability to experience consciousness. The spiritualist Elkhart Tolle describes "choice" as "implying consciousness and without it, you have no choice."[10] In the present speed of life, many of our choices are made in a split second and without consciousness.

This is the nature of addiction, choice without consciousness. Any of our human wants can, with the right environment (externally and internally), proceed on the continuum of a quest for pleasure and pain relief, especially when we have a genetic predisposition to the sensitivity of a substance disorder.

SOCIAL IMPACT

Not professing to be a sociologist, I can only share what I have experienced and learned about social changes that may be influencing environmental risk factors for substance use disorders. For instance, incidences of childhood abuse and trauma greatly accelerate the likelihood of developing substance addictions. Also influencing increased substance use, misuse, and abuse are the following:

- **The speed of life continues to accelerate.** Everything is more instantaneous: communication; the global economy; financial transactions; product specialization, advertising, marketing, purchasing, and delivery; and news, entertainment and information spread. This speed change, as an outgrowth of rapid technological advances, has both great advantages and unintentional consequences, such as less time for thinking, resting, relaxing, self-introspection, choice, and just the consciousness of being present. Personal connection, therefore relationships with our own being, others, and the universe have suffered from so much device and other busy time.

- **Consumerism has become a poor substitute for real connection**. But it is flourishing in our search for external satisfaction and meaning, too often through instant gratifications like pleasures, power, and possessions. We seek the external to try to assuage our internal needs and angst.

    The best-selling book, *Dopamine Nation*, carries a subtitle, "Finding Balance in the Age of Indulgence." In it, Dr. Anna Lembke describes "our moment of wanting" as "the brain's pleasure balance tipped to the side of pain." She suggests that the way we find balance is combining the science of desire with the wisdom of recovery "to rediscover our genuine self in the midst of our 'wanting' the outside fix."[11]

    In recovery, we are taught that our fears, angers, and resentments rise when we either don't get what we want or we are afraid of losing what we have. The consumerism of today is a fear and stress generator chasing our increased desires and consequently obsessive tendencies.

- **"Existential threats" to human safety and survival are present to us more than ever.** The increased threats are both because of their reality and because we are bombarded by the mention of them daily through the twenty-four-hour news media and our addiction to devices.

    We have clear and present dangers that cause considerable angst, in spite of our efforts to muzzle them. These threats to our being involve global and space wars; criminal gangs and upsurges of general and random violence; air pollution levels advancing global warming with life-threatening storms, fires, flooding, famines, droughts, and disappearing islands and coastlines; aggressive and impaired drivers on our roads; substances that, when used improperly, can kill almost instantly; bridges collapsing; and oh yeah, the capacity of so many secret government and nongovernment entities to hack massive databases and send long-range spy balloons, missiles, and nuclear warheads anywhere and quickly, even into space. It's no wonder existential threats create more fears and internal stress for us.

- **Significant and relatively recent changes in contemporary family structures have resulted in more parental absence.** Increased divorce rates, single parent households, and two parents working lead to less parental time and influence on children and adolescents. Dr. Maté claims today "dislocation" disrupts family life and erodes stable communities, concluding that "a sense of emptiness and loneliness pervade our culture." He references nutrition, physical security, and emotional nurturing as the three essentials to an optimal childhood and claims that emotional nurturing is "most likely to be disrupted in Western societies."[12]

He also refers to an article in the Drug and Alcohol Dependence journal specifying this trend toward "lost attachment relationships of children to be the strongest social factor in the age of onset and early escalation of adolescent substance use."[13]

For many kids with minimal or absentee parenting and adult role models, Dr. Maté says their substitute of choice for guidance and direction is often obtained from "peer affiliation," a term coined by psychologist Gordon Neufeld. At a life stage when child and adolescent brains are undeveloped, vulnerability to risk-taking is higher and feeling invincible is the norm. Looking to peers, "peer affiliation," is a dangerous source of guidance and often a cause for shutting down emotionally.

Kids, as a rule, not only lack the problem-solving capacity to grasp a model of maturity, they lack the actual life experiences to learn, from which many life lessons develop. Peer affiliation combined with a child's feelings of emotional alienation or abandonment make for a risk-filled environmental setting.

It has been my experience that physically and emotionally absent parents have a tendency to show up in their kid's life just often enough to either shower them with material gifts or money; often blame others, like teachers, for their offspring's immature behaviors; or set verbal expectations for the child without providing much real training and experience to help their kid to grow into maturity.

- **Adolescent drinking alcohol at a younger age than previous generations is a major indicator leading to future alcohol misuse and other substance use.** Young people mimic their adult counterparts. Our social mass media marketing and public event experiences inform young people that drinking is the adult way of having fun.

  According to the National Institute on Alcohol Abuse and Addiction, for most children, drinking alcohol is the first risky behavior tried. Alcohol is, by far, the drug of choice among youth. One in three children start drinking by the end of eighth grade and nearly one in four by their senior year of high school. The sad fact is that heavy drinking in youth can result in long-lasting functional and structural changes in the brain.[14]

  Here again, the legal drugs of alcohol, tobacco, and now marijuana are obvious gateway substances for more risk-taking. Our society is currently promoting the acceptability of these adult "pleasures," but once kids move to more risky, perhaps lethal drugs, we ostracize them and stigmatize them as "druggies," (or similar negative labeling) designating them as outcasts on the periphery of society. I find considerable hypocrisy in condemning what we socially promote. One new example of this hypocritical attitude is legalizing recreational marijuana use and then subsequently raising concerns about the evident spike in impaired driving and accidents.

- **There is an increasing loss of public confidence in our previously trusted institutions.** This mistrust is of our government, politics, judicial system, law enforcement, media, business and corporations, employers, communications, public health, food industry, education and even our religious organizations. Widespread doubt also stems from our absence of real interpersonal connections. Who can we count on? Is our wellbeing at issue?

The decline of general public trust and isolation from other people has resulted in a widespread sense of personal alienation, abandonment, a certain level of predictability to life and often a general societal divide accompanied by frustration, anger and resentment for "others". Others are anyone who looks different, thinks differently and comes from a different place and perspective.

Hostility becomes the weapon when difference is not resolved, whether by institutional process or individual relationships. Gaps in perspective among society have widened in many public arenas. Middle ground is hard to find in these deep schisms of a tribal mentality aimed at social, economic, medical, justice and other public issues including religious and spiritual separation.

Too much or too little government? A deep state? Fair elections? Border control? Who do we let in? How do we defend our country and our own existence and freedom? Open or close? The role of parents, schools, science, medicine, pharmacology and churches? Differences are multiplying and angst is the product, even fear.

Our lifestyles are becoming more fear based. Technology, globalization, disease, diversity, science and industry are among the major factors that have rapidly changed how we see the world in just the last few years. All is up for grabs today.

With the increased stress and anxiety of such accelerated change and uncertainty, our desire for pleasure and pain relief are heightened considerably. I believe all of this adds up to the accompanying increase in substance misuse with its growing disease rates.

- **It used to be that religion and churches were where we would go to seek peace, comfort and comradery, as a salve for our souls.** Today, unlike the early communal Christian church I find many to be in the battlefield of doctrinal sanctity. Political correctness is yielding to the rise of spiritual correctness. Love, compassion and tolerance often fall prey to folks who think they have the appointed wisdom on how God thinks, what he means by his Word and what others should believe.

Thank God, in recovery we have a concept where we each identify our own Higher Power. It is strongly suggested we don't let our pride manifest itself as a terminal uniqueness and limited mindset. We don't accept or dictate what others must accept as the Truth.

One of my very favorite books about spirituality is <u>Your God Is Too Small</u>, a classic written by J. B. Phillips. In it he suggests that no human being has the inside track on the Word, that an omnipotent, omniscient and omnipresent deity has a capacity that "passes all understanding".[15] Is God "big" enough for our world today?

My point is that in our world of conflict, we now have difficulty looking for a spiritually correct church or institution and yet spiritual connection is one of our primary human evolutionary goals. We can look to substances for relief, and we are. Or we can find our own spiritual path and reconnect with other people, serve others without the judgement and doctrinal sanctity that adds to our divisions and contributes to creating more self-centered fear.

- **Addiction care is avoided or takes a back seat in our public health system and mainstream medicine.** Public health insurers, governmental and private, as well as medical schools are also significant contributors to the issue of inadequate substance addiction care.

    The ability of individuals to obtain help is contingent upon factors such as adequate funding levels, payer fee structures, navigable assessment treatment enrollment processes and the quality of care provided. Finding affordable, available and accessible assistance from trained professionals can be puzzling. Receiving a welcoming invitation without being judged or treated indifferently is not always the norm. Public policy makers and insurance payers could work together to make the entire care experience much more understandable, predictable, consistent and customer friendly.

A GLIMPSE OF THE OPPONENT

My goal in life from early childhood has always been to become … an alcoholic! Really??? When was the last time you heard anyone express their life's ambition to become an addict or alcoholic? No one in their right mind dreams of such shame and imprisonment! Many of us thought "it won't happen to me." I am too smart, too industrious, too goal-driven, too invulnerable, and too emotionally tough to let a simple substance control me. Yet here I am with millions of others just like me! In my case, the suffering from my years of alcohol use has been the primary, long-term symptom of my own journey to "free myself from the bondage of the Self."

Had I not received help from a welcoming and compassionate recovery community twenty-five years ago, I would have unquestionably faced even more of the inevitable destructive outcomes nearly all untreated alcoholics or addicts eventually experienced. I have also been so fortunate to have several mentors who have taught me both the basics of recovery itself and the neurological brain science behind the disease.

By the way, in a recent alcohol recovery program study, the Twelve Step recovery methodology pioneered by Alcoholics Anonymous (AA) in 1935 was comparatively considered the most effective abstinence program presently operating around the globe.[16]

Unfortunately, even with twelve-step programs, the less than 10 percent rate of new members staying sober for one year is frustratingly low. At the same time, the percentage of new adults with substance use disorders entering any recovery programs or communities is equally disappointing. And the numbers and percentages of people becoming addicted to legal mind-altering substances continue to grow. Most young people who become addicted to illegal, life threatening substances like fentanyl, start their early experimentation with legal drugs.

THE FUNDAMENTALS OF ADDICTION PHYSIOLOGY

To me, one of the most fascinating revelations that motivated me to better understand my alcohol misuse and write about it is the fact that my physiology differences made me more prone to becoming addicted.

The biological reasons that we drink or use drugs: to gain pleasure or relieve pain.

Characteristics of Substance Use Disorders – it is the primary disease, not a subset of other physical, psychological or mental illnesses

- Chronic – capable of being placed into remission but not curable
- Progressive – symptoms worsen with continued drinking or use
- Fatal – if untreated, through premature consequences

Predictable outcomes of Substance Use Disorder (if untreated)

- Progressively adverse consequences – mental, spiritual, social, emotional, spousal, family and financial
- Incarceration or institutionalization or premature death by accident, suicide or violence
- Brain and body dysfunction and illnesses (e.g., heart, digestion, cancer, liver, skeletal, central nervous system)

The Three Laws of Pharmacology[17] that apply to all mind-altering chemicals

- Chemicals that enter the body affect the brain by speeding up or slowing down its rate of activity
- The brain creates its own chemicals to create a counter-reaction to the initial brain rate effect of the external chemical intake
- With continued external chemical use the ongoing repetitive counter-balancing processes attempted by the brain result in its dysfunction and damaging structural changes

The primary risk factors that lead to Substance Use Disorder

- Genetic predisposition and epigenetic influences
- The availability of the substance
- Environment, including pre-natal, post-natal influences and trauma
- Age of onset (first substance use)

The three cyclical stages of SUD

- Tolerance change
- Withdrawal – acute or protracted
- Craving phenomenon

Examples of individual physiological differences causing increased likelihood of addiction are described in detail later in the book but include level of cellular sensitivity, ability of the liver to metabolize ethanol faster than normal, insufficient or loss of dopamine production in the brain and sensitivity to stress and variances in cortisol production.

WHO ARE WE FAILING TODAY?

The obvious, most publicized group is our young people dying from illegal drug overdoses. The catastrophic consequences are shocking, easily visible, and devastating to families and communities. Some health care systems and providers, and schools are grasping, however anemically, to respond to this crisis. Rightly so. Much more effort is needed. Remember, with young people their underdeveloped brains allow risk-taking behaviors, and the first substance they likely use is a legal or soon-to-be legal one that is easily accessible to them.

Other groups we are failing (as documented by national data) because we do not have a comprehensive, regulated, and accountable mainstream medical collaborative care system for substance disorders are women, seniors, veterans, middle class professionals and working-class employees and their employers, among others. Remember, fewer than one in twenty individuals with substance misuse or use disorder ever get any help for their disease, let alone receive quality care.

What can writing this book do to help? Our goal is to educate you about the modern medical disease model of addiction and the basic physiology of alcohol and substance use disorders. You will learn how this chronic, progressive disease has affected my life and my family, as well as others.

We provide details on the disease of addiction, its progression and effect on the brain and body. This material comes from over a decade of research and numerous sources are given; it's a great reference for those who want to dive deeper.

We share with you what we believe constitutes the best practices of recovery: a high quality, comprehensive collaborative care model and relapse prevention.

We explain why we consider family disease education and support, as well as early patient integration into twelve-step programs, or other recovery support group environments, of great importance.

In Volume II I will share with you some ideas I used with addiction patients in my "Coach's Corner" chalk talks about what "a practical spirituality" means, how it relates to addiction recovery, and how each person benefits in recovery from choosing and growing their own individual spiritual path.

Lastly, we can offer the outline of a new vision for community health with mainstream medical practices serving as primary entry points to managed networks of addiction care. We can reach "more, broader, earlier, kinder, faster, better, longer" (and oh yes, more cost effective)!

A DIRECT CHALLENGE TO MAINSTREAM MEDICAL PRACTICE DOCTORS

This section is directed to **Family Practice Docs, Pediatricians, Emergency Care Workers, Internal Medicine Docs, and Other Prescribers with Regular Patient Flow.**

PRE-SEASON PREPARATION

You are the medical professionals who can reform addiction care in this country. Under the current situation, very few individuals with a legal alcohol or other substance use problem are identified, let alone helped or given quality care. Doctors have difficulty with conditions they cannot measure precisely and have no comparative norms for diagnosis and treatment.

Since most of you are not screening your existing patients on a routine basis for this disease, the few sufferers who do get help mostly enter a "rehab" system without protections, enforced regulations, and care standards. Or individuals erroneously begin to seek help through therapy.

Regardless of the often legitimate reasons for your hesitancy, providing initial addiction screening, early intervention and a referral to quality, proven, accountable treatment providers is key. You have a primary responsibility to begin addressing earlier identification of patients with the number one medical issue facing your share of the public. Why you? Because you are in the best possible position to be an entry point for healing, to start a person on the path to recovery!

We recommend the adoption of the Screening, Brief Intervention, and Referral To Treatment (SBIRT) program for initial screening and care to earlier detect and help patients with a potential alcohol or substance use disorder.

Numerous studies of SBIRT around the globe in the last ten years have clearly demonstrated significant positive patient results for adults, women, seniors, adolescents, young adults, and active-duty military personnel. The overwhelming consensus in the US, Europe, Great Britain, and China have found SBIRT "an effective, affordable, widely implementable intervention tool to reduce misuse rates, disorder rates, alcohol and other substance consumption. In addition, reductions of drug use, inpatient hospitalizations, primary care visits, depression, psychiatric visits, and SUD diagnoses were documented, while more medicine-assisted treatment was recorded."

It is not nuclear physics to screen patients with the SBIRT methodology; it's straightforward to grasp the concepts, techniques, and processes to administer the necessary tools. A list of SBIRT best practices is presented in the appendix.

Here is a summary of what we need from you, our mainstream medical and dental professionals, to help lower the incidence of more fully developed, substance use disorders and to significantly lower relapse rates of your identified patients:

- Implement SBIRT (Screening, Brief Intervention, and Referral To Treatment) for the legal substances—alcohol, marijuana or cannabis, and prescription drug misuse
- Link SBIRT to an available and easily accessible proven quality provider for assessment, diagnosis, treatment, and disease education
- Link SUD (Substance Use Disorder) diagnosed patients with chronic care management, peer support, and monitoring for at least two years after successful treatment

FOR PUBLIC AND PRIVATE INSURANCE PAYERS

You too can do your part to save dollars and lives in the long run by initially providing fair, equitable, and predictable fees for the time spent by mainstream doctors and office practice champions to utilize SBIRT. You can also participate in the development and implementation of value-added fee incentives for both attaining performance measurements and utilizing peer coaching / monitoring services after initial treatment that are proven to reduce relapse rates and save further treatment costs.

The eventual cost savings for supporting preventative screening and initial intervention strategies, as well as supporting recovery support teams for coaching, follow-up, monitoring, and rewarding patient/provider performance progress will more than offset the certain future costs for the majority of patients who relapse in year one after expensive, but often insufficient treatment and monitoring.

A path to recovery begins with the acceptance of the problem and the willingness to ask for help. Existing mainstream medical practices are the best-positioned catalysts to turn on the switch, to light up step one of the recovery process. Fee payers can play a significant role in building into the recovery process those best practices that lower relapse rates and longer term financial waste.

"More, Broader, Kinder, Earlier, Faster, Better, Longer!"

THE GAME:
COACH'S STORY

1945: GENETIC PREDISPOSITION

A telegram from the US Army command in Europe reached the thirty-four-week pregnant wife of a soldier in Ohio on Christmas Eve 1944. The news was bad and couldn't have been more poorly timed. Her husband, my Dad, serving as an enlisted scout in the Longneck 274th Armored Field Artillery Battalion under General George Patton, was hit by German shrapnel in the Battle of the Bulge and flown to a London hospital for surgery in critical condition.

Not knowing whether her husband and the father of her soon-to-be baby was alive or dead, Mom courageously delivered me, her first of two boys, on January 4, 1945. It was not until March of '45 that word reached her in the States that surgery on her husband had been successful, leaving him with a slight limp, a Purple heart, and other medals for his service.

What I have since surprisingly learned later in my study of substance use disorders is that this situation was the first in a series of what I will refer to as "unintentionally afflicted prenatal trauma" on Mom, and consequently, on me in her womb. No one at that time was aware that prenatal and postnatal events could have a significant influence upon an emotional life and discreetly produce a sense of alienation I would carry into my later adulthood. Let me explain.

Dad received his Purple Heart in a London hospital and was returned to his US Army artillery unit in Germany for their final march against the Reich. Because he had taken trigonometry in high school, Dad was assigned to be a forward scout. His unit ended up being the first American troops to emancipate two prison camps, Bergen-Belsen and Buchenwald. Later, to my son, his grandson, Dad related his recollection of the harrowing experiences from which he would never forget the odor of burning bodies from miles around the camps.

Like many other soldiers who have experienced war and returned home, he was extremely hesitant to discuss his experiences, as if he had left his home, his life, and had been projected onto another planet where chaos was rampant, and hell was visibly encountered. He was a hero to us but, other than staying in touch with a few of his close outfit buddies over the years, he preferred to try to forget the war. Dad focused his energies as best he could on working, raising a family, building a career, and building life itself again.

Although abandoned before birth by his own alcoholic father, he was raised by his mother, with his uncle's help, to live a hardworking and Christian lifestyle. As a returning soldier and father, he set out to raise his family with love, discipline, and industriousness.

It was a comfortable, safe environment for my brother and I to grow up in, where education, hard work, and responsibility were stressed. My stay-at-home mother demonstrated and taught love, care, and being kind to others, especially less fortunate people. It was a good combination! In this "Wally Cleaver" home of the 1950s to '60s, part of our family life was centered on church activities. Both of us boys were exposed to Bible study, Sunday school and regular worship at an early age.

However, our clear and primary interest, the continuing passion for both of us, was sports—football, basketball, baseball, and track, depending on the season. Neither of our parents approved of drinking, smoking, gambling, or swearing. We were too busy playing ball to get into much trouble, except for the occasional broken lamp from a ball thrown wildly in our living room. Also, I can't recall an official athletic contest of mine or my younger brother that either of my parents missed.

I remember making a makeshift track-and-field stadium in our backyard one spring. For the pole vault, we used a laundry pole and an existing clothesline to be the crossbar we tried to vault over. I remember one day when Mom came running out toward us from the backdoor of the house screaming, "Gregory Wince, if you or your brother gets killed trying that foolish stunt, don't come running to me!"

There were many moments like that when our common sense gave way to using our yard (or front room on rainy days) for a playground of makeshift sports arenas. Often guys from all over town would show up to play in our driveway or yard.

We made an undersized baseball field from which balls would land in neighbors' yards and gardens, against their garages, and worse yet, occasionally shattering their windows. The same "accidents" occurred when we mowed a golf course in the grass all around our house to hold our invitational golf tournaments with real golf balls. Yep! More thumps and shattered glass. Oh well! We were mostly wise enough to initiate these "accidents" when Dad was at work or the church.

Mom was a good soul. She taught me to care for others and be compassionate, polite, and always help people less fortunate. I'm sure her concern and compassion for others came from her own experiences as a child growing up in the Great Depression era. Mom's father left home, leaving her mother and six daughters ranging from four to twelve years old. Mom lived both with her aunt and in the local Children's Home for a couple of her early years before her mom could afford to get all the girls back together in the same tight-knit family household.

As a young lady, Mom was both a gifted singer and loved sports, playing basketball in an era when female athletes were rare. After high school, she studied music in Chicago, then came home, married, and became a "Rosie the Riveter" in the World War II years. In church she sang solos, and the one with the words I most remember was "Brighten the Corner Where You Are!" When she was well, that was Mom! I can hear her singing now in her melodic soprano voice calling to me to "brighten the corner where you are."

Aside from her prenatal and postnatal trauma related to Dad's war injury and the threat of losing him, my mother suffered chronic back pain and had to regularly undergo traction treatments in the hospital. And she underwent four traumatic and lengthy surgical stays in Columbus hospitals. As a result, she was often away from home or bedridden with depression, and I believe she developed recurrent drug dependency to routinely prescribed painkillers like Percocet and Valium.

Fortunately, my dad's mother, Granny, lived with us and did more than her share to keep our household operating and us boys out of trouble while Mom was disabled. Granny must have been a religiously born-again terror when she was younger. Her rules were clear: no drinking, no smoking, no swearing, no card playing, no sex, and no ideas about any of the above!

As a cleaning lady with several jobs at a time, Granny (my wife referred to her as the "Little Old Lady from Pasadena" after a popular rock 'n' roll song) never missed giving a weekly tithe minimum of 10 percent of her meager earnings to the church. Volunteering as the chief cook and clean-up person at every church event held for years, Granny lived to be 105 years old and was helping by delivering meals on wheels to "those old people," as she referred to them, until she was 97. She lived a very humble, servant life. However, "the Nos" she tried to teach me all went out the window as soon as the "evil reared its ugly head of temptation" opportunities presented themselves to me as an adolescent. I was the stereotypical "rebellious child," predisposed genetically to an early age of onset and a physiological and environmental risk to potentially develop substance use disorder.

My father worked his way up from a letter carrier to be the superintendent of the local US post office and served in that capacity for nearly thirty years. The habit of walking he developed on his mail-delivery job became a permanent one, even a passion for him. With that slight limp he walked everywhere he could. Often daily and regardless of the weather, he walked to and from work, a five-mile trek each way. He also walked the neighborhood almost every evening. Sometimes, I think his evening walks were, for him, an escape from seeing the suffering Mom was experiencing. We called him the Walking Man.

Dad was a volunteer sheriff's deputy and little league baseball officer, an active political party member, as well as the church trustee board president, church treasurer, and an adult Sunday school teacher for years. He was a curious learner, a self-taught Biblical scholar, and he was fascinated with astronomy and Carl Sagan's work. A pillar of our community until he retired in his late sixties, Dad was an admired, respected, steady, dependable, and very industrious family man until, as an elderly man, he became heart-breakingly lost, sick, and confused.

In his late sixties, my father, like so many aging men, began to feel isolated without continuing to work and feeling productive. He began to socialize with a group of friends, several WWII vets at lunch. Having not drank alcohol since his youth, Dad had a martini, then two, four, or more daily. Drinking quickly activated his genetic predisposition for alcohol. His disorder progressed rapidly, as seniors often are accelerated in a late life manifestation of an alcohol use disease.

After wrecking his car several times and somehow finding a set of car keys, even after five sets were confiscated and hidden from him, he passed away from heart complications. Sadly, he died after a few spiraling, chaotic years of drinking, continually refusing to admit he had any sort of drinking problem, even when he was professionally assessed and positively diagnosed. Alcohol had worked very quickly on him at his elderly age.

The memories of him are still confusing today. For decades he was the model of stability, consistency, and dependability, Then, for the last few years of his life, we watched him with agony, feeling helpless and with a sense of panic, at his lack of control as he destroyed himself with drink. Could I please just remember Dad before he got sick? Time, years, and disease knowledge have helped.

Yet, like every other alcoholic or addict, regardless of what age you start, what religion you practice, what work history you've earned, or the family you are from, if you have the genetic predisposition like my father and I have, once you activate your disease and feed it, the addiction process begins. It just happened so much more quickly for a senior like Dad. While my father was moving through the disease stages at a seemingly mercurial speed, I was quietly sloshing my way along my own chaotic path of being enveloped by booze.

MY TURN: CHILDHOOD TRAUMA AND THE AGE OF ONSET

My uncle, who helped raise my father, owned and operated a busy restaurant-bar in a small town forty miles east of my hometown. On one of our regular family overnight visits there on Friday evenings, at age thirteen, I drank my first beer with my cousin. Researchers would label this introduction to alcohol as my "age of onset," the date I started drinking. The taste was strange, but the feeling "warm."

Like most young people who begin to experiment with alcohol, this was the beginning of a new path to a different social life. It was, in my inexperienced perspective, an expedient route to adulthood. Like many young people find, drinking and smoking cigarettes promoted the false pretense of maturity and coolness. Additionally, I began to develop a taste for alcohol and a growing attraction for that uninhibited euphoric feeling of imbibing. Some in recovery call this process trying to "fill the hole in your soul." At an early age, due to several painful experiences of social isolation, my lonely soul was aching to be filled!

At age nine, I contracted rheumatic fever which was introduced to me and my family as potentially fatal. My whole life and source of pleasure were built around a passionate interest in sports. This disease curtailed my athletic participation, my passion and primary source of self-expression for several years. Although my grades in school remained impeccable, I felt lost, left out of normal life. My dreams of being an athlete were being shattered by an unexpected, uncontrollable health condition attacking my normal heart function and my joints.

Fortunately, two years later my doctor allowed me to resume playing baseball, but no other more strenuous sports. A partial reprieve, I was reunited with friends in at least one area of athletics and competed effectively in academics and baseball for a couple of years.

All was well with my world until it wasn't. A sense of alienation and a recognition of my mortality came back with a vengeance! The summer before tenth grade, my first year attending a very large high school, I was diagnosed with a rare form of leukemia with no available cure and transported to the children's cancer ward in the Ohio State University Hospital. There I spent several unforgettably stressful, emotional-filled months expecting the worst.

Most experts believe that a severe childhood physical or emotional trauma can be, along with genetics, a major risk factor in the development of a substance use disorder. This experience in the hospital was, for me, fearful and disheartening, forever etched in my memory. This period in my life became an emotional trigger of psychologically traumatic feelings of alienation.

In the first week of my hospital stay, my roommate, Thad H., died, of Hodgkin's Disease, in our room in the middle of the night. I remember watching intently, frozen in place as they lifted him onto a cart and removed him.

My parents visited me daily, and I could often see or hear them weeping after consulting medical staff. Visitors, my classmates, and church members showed up to cheer me up and ended up sobbing and holding me.

I will never forget that totally out-of-control feeling of being trapped without any tangible recourse. By the third month in the hospital, I believe I was the only child still living among those young patients who were there on the same ward when I was admitted. The darkness hovered, and I saw no way out. Sad does not describe the events that occurred during my extended stay! My life and any involvement in sports at home disappeared. In fact, my life itself seemed to be disappearing.

In recovery from addiction, there is a saying that "God did for me what I could not do for myself." Although I cannot prove this tenet, I have to admit this phenomenon has occurred in my life more than once at several vital times, including during this ongoing and traumatic nightmare

I can clearly recall that bright Autumn morning in early October. The doctors and med students were making their normal morning rounds. Yet, as they filed into my room that morning, they were uncharacteristically smiling and several had tears in their eyes. The lead physician joyously informed my parents and me that what they initially thought was leukemia (because of my abnormal white blood cell count), was in fact, a newly discovered, infectious "kissing disease" known as mononucleosis! I wasn't dying! Oh, my!

So how sick was I? My prognosis instantly changed from the dark of night to glimpses of sunshine. We were advised that after an extensive bed rest for several months at home, I would be able to return to school and resume a relatively normal life … except. The exception, of course, was another prohibition of my athletic participation, as a health precaution.

Having my life back was monumental and I was so grateful, but I did not realize how much this entire experience, including another lengthy period of social isolation, would impact my emotional well-being in the immediate future and my overall health in the long run. These childhood traumas impacted my reality and psyche more than I realized then.

I was tutored at home for months; my regularly assigned high school teachers came to visit me twice a week after school. Because of their availability and devotion, I was able to catch up academically and maintained top grades in each subject. I was back to being physically in attendance at the high school the following late spring. Unfortunately, resuming normalcy to my life was not in practical reach. Too much change had impacted my young formative soul and my less than fully developed brain! I had been cheerful and briefly encouraged with the direction of my life momentarily, but the reality began to cut me into little pieces.

EXPERIMENTAL/RECREATIONAL USE

The transition to rejoin my classmates in an unfamiliar, large school campus facility, new teachers, most of the students being strangers, was challenging and emotionally uncomfortable. This intimidating environment in which I was entering had the second largest high school enrollment in the state. Not being permitted to rejoin my buddies who were participating in sports was even more disheartening. I felt lonely and estranged, out of place.

My father, rightly so, was concerned about me having too much spare time without sports and urged me to find part-time work. I became a clerk in a downtown shoe store after school and on Saturdays. It was through this job that I became quite familiar with the downtown pool hall scene and a different group of associates. I was becoming resentful and discontented with a whole new reality thrust upon me. Work was a poor and humdrum substitute for my athletic desires.

The downtown pool room environment was also, unfortunately, a real-life laboratory for my new experiments of smoking, drinking, and gambling. In an environment of new acquaintances, I was able to increase my access to alcohol and did so. Some of the older poolroom veterans would buy the beer or whiskey and smokes for us underage blossoming "men." Oh, we got trouble!

I had discovered a part-time escape route from loneliness and boredom, an accessible path to some social connection, and what projected to be a newfound feeling of adulthood. My grades began to drop, and although I graduated with honors, I undoubtedly missed out on more recognition and scholarships. I grew very apathetic toward school and felt alone, vulnerable in the "real world," without sports and competing with a team.

In our senior year of high school, a buddy of mine and I decided to skip school every Wednesday and drive to a college campus, where we had friends, about a half hour from home. It was our way of breaking up the mundane week, drinking a little beer, and checking out the college coeds. While I had plenty of academic cushion to graduate in June, my buddy, unfortunately, was forced to go to summer school to get his diploma.

Leaving high school marked the rather innocent and benign beginning of unintended consequences for me and those around me because of my increasing social involvement with drinking and its associated behaviors. The consequences silently started to pile up with my search for pleasure and relief from emotional angst. College would become the perfect environment to meet other binge drinkers and turn the experimental use of alcohol into a growing intoxication habit.

THE BINGE/INTOXICATION STAGE

College, Family, and Two Full-Time Careers

Frail physically and over a year younger than most of my classmates, I weighed 150 pounds when I graduated from high school. A close friend of mine decided to attend a university in northern Ohio, and I decided to follow suit. The landscape there was flat, the weather cold, and the wind constant.

My attitude toward college mirrored the climate. I wanted to be a coach and didn't see the necessity for classes not devoted directly to this end. I was homesick and began to binge drink on weekends to escape loneliness. Studying was an afterthought. So much for getting off to the strong academic start I planned, and my parents expected.

Between weekend binges and hanging out with the student union pool tables, I lifted weights, practiced basketball, and played intramural sports. Physically I matured rapidly, catching up with my peers in size and strength.

On a fall evening at one of my intramural basketball games, two university basketball team assistant coaches happened to observe the contest. I made most of my shots that night. To my real surprise, one of the coaches extended me an invitation to join the college freshman team, complete with free and better meals at the university's athletic training table. Of course, I unhesitatingly accepted and immediately went into overdrive to get in shape by running up and down the dormitory steps, before, after, and sometimes during classes!

I was so relieved and excited to be on a team again. Finally, after the years of disappointment and alienation from not participating in athletics, out of nowhere, I was rescued. I was motivated. I was ecstatic. I belonged! I Mattered!

Although I did not play a lot of minutes, I practiced, traveled, ate, and socialized with the team and its scholarship athletes. Our varsity had two guys, Nate Thurmond and Howard Komives, who later became NBA stars. They led the team into the NCAA tournament and afforded me my initial experience at getting to attend March Madness up close. I was playing among the stars!

Being on the team, I had my choice of fraternities and pledged that winter with several other players. I felt like I fit in, and I socialized with athletes and other guys who liked to party. On weekends and after weekday home games we roamed the downtown college bars and clubs, of course at the expense of my academics. I was playing among the stars! When I left campus after that freshman year, I knew my chances of making the varsity squad the following year were slim and wondered how I would be able to cope again on that campus without being active on the team.

The decision of how I would cope was made for me! My father, who received a copy of my less-than-favorable grade report, decided I needed to come home, work, and earn my own money as well as attend night classes at a community college near home. My thrill of a lifetime came to an abrupt halt! I begrudgingly went home.

Packing lawnmowers by placing them into boxes for shipment at the end of the conveyor belt or cleaning out the hot ovens at a local glass-wool factory were not my idea of a promising career. I quickly rekindled the urge to return to college.

Before I was able to do that—nearly a year—my life was drink, work, sleep, drink. Several of the guys I befriended in the factory stopped in neighborhood bars after work and sometimes before shift time. I fit with that agenda.

These were guys who liked to drink like me. They were clear examples of drinkers who built an increased tolerance for alcohol and could consume drink after drink before stopping. The factory softball team also became another excellent source for my "tolerance-building." Oh, I got friends!

That summer, I decided to enroll at a small, private college about thirty miles from home. I knew several students who attended there, and they sold the attractiveness of their small school environment to me. Excited to be escaping my parental oversight at home and receiving a second chance at an education, I gladly surrendered the monotony of factory work.

I felt much more comfortable with the small school atmosphere, and my initial grades were respectable. And I became very physically fit, now tipping the scales at 195. Joining a local fraternity, I became friends with a number of athletes who urged me to play their sports. So instead of playing basketball, as I originally intended, I ended up playing baseball and football.

My closest friends were my teammates and other frat guys who liked to drink like me. As an upperclassman, I continued to skip a lot of classes but luckily obtained enough credits and a minimum GPA to qualify for graduation. I was the first in my family to earn a degree.

A very positive event for me occurred at college in my senior year. Woody Hayes, the famous Ohio State football coach, came to speak at a chapel on campus. After his speech, I introduced myself to him and told him I was an aspiring coach and had read as many coaching books as I could find. Little did I know this would lead to a beneficial affiliation with him.

Coach Hayes invited me to his office several times, which led to long, but fascinating three- to five-hour discussions, and mostly one-way conversations about coaching and, the history and strategies of war. Occasionally on Friday evenings the coach and/or his wife Anne would drive from their home in Upper Arlington east to Newcomerstown, and pick me up on their way at the corner of Route 161 and Cleveland Avenue in Columbus. Then they would drop me off in Newark, so I could see my brother play high school football.

Later in life, Coach Hayes agreed to be my cochair when I was appointed as Licking County Census Chairman. He was very gracious and helpful in recording publicly broadcast interviews urging people to be counted as US citizens and residents. He also accepted and honored my request to speak at a national conference our organization helped sponsor in Columbus for hundreds of high school dropouts returning to complete their basic education and skill training. He never said no to helping me with what he considered meaningful service. I imagine he was like that with many others as well.

Apart from his successful coaching career and behind-the-scenes volunteer work, I know he had his faults. But Coach Hayes was one of my true heroes and a great example of the kind of coach and person I wanted to be. Demanding, but serving others.

I was inspired by other coaches, but not enough to shelve alcohol. It allowed me to act out without feeling the angst I carried about life and its responsibilities. Although relatively harmless, my frat brothers and I were occasionally reckless with mischievous behavior.

One night while sufficiently inebriated, four of us decided to "borrow" the university president's Volkswagen Beetle from his driveway and deposit it on the steps behind the student union. Unfortunately, three of the four of us were caught—me, I was the lucky fugitive. The unlucky three received school discipline. A couple of years later, I was startled to observe one of these buddies starring in a leading role on "Days of Our

Lives" and acting in national television commercials. Handsome guy, darn good tackle, but a more successful actor and theater director. The other three of us became teacher-coaches after we finished college.

During my senior year at Otterbein, I met a dark-haired, brown-eyed beauty named Bev who had returned to her alma mater to work on a National Institute of Health (NIH) genetics project in the science department. She had the most lovable cocker spaniel, and between the girl and her dog, I was smitten. I later became engaged to this dark-haired beauty who happened to be smart and mature.

My buddies were adamant she would never go out with me—too good looking and way too smart for me. I knew I stood in a long line, but she did agree to spend an evening with me and we fell in love almost immediately.

Bev was the top woman scholar in her college graduating class and had spent the prior year in a genetics research lab at Johns Hopkins Hospital in Baltimore. I, due to drinking and being immature, was her opposite academically.

As resistant as I was to academic studying, I was quite obsessed with reading every book I could find on football and basketball coaching. My fiancé tried to refocus me enough to ensure I graduated. She did help to some degree, especially in anatomy, physiology, and kinesiology classes.

But she also represented what real responsibility and maturity exemplified, and there wasn't much latitude in her world for me when she had to experience what became my more frequent drinking binges.

She and I had many common interests, the bonds that I think saved our engagement and marriage several times over the years when we encountered rough seas due to my self-centered fear and addiction behaviors. She tried to cope but was sometimes forced to swim in my alcohol disease.

Eventually, she found her own path to serenity through Al-Anon, a twelve-step support group for spouses and friends of individuals with substance use disorders. Throughout the many years of her participation in this wonderful group, she helped so many others who were exposed to the disease with a loved one. Thank God we both loved children, sports, dogs, and each of us valued our spiritual interests. We both have been so fortunate to find recovery from this family disease. We learned over time to accept and love each other the way we are.

When I was dating her, I tried to contain my drinking but would invariably find the inopportune times to binge. To facilitate my escape into alcohol, I would start arguments with her or tell her we were getting "too close" for comfort, and I needed "space" from dating. This "fight and flee" habit lasted off and on for too many years. It was my way to escape from myself and drink in isolation. I could avoid feeling vulnerable and cover up my deep-seated fear of inadequacy and potential alienation. What kind of a fool was I to gamble on losing her for alcohol?

I found out much later that this is typical of someone with a substance use disorder, using behavioral defense mechanisms to create "space" for drinking and to fabricate a sense of internal justification.

Space was really my escape based upon a fear of intimacy and responsibility. I was learning to wallow in self-pity, anger, and resentment. Embracing the delusion that I deserved time to drink, I was merely using what the recovery program refers to as pity: "poor me, poor me, pour me a drink." Rationalization, justification, and transference were defense mechanisms I learned to practice to perfection over many years. My behavior kept our relationship on the rocks too often.

Predictably after I indulged in a temporary binge "fix," I would run back to my wife pleading, "I'm sorry," and wanting to be instantly reunited, forgiven like a little lost hungover puppy. The routine of fight or flight became a staple in my subconscious strategy to escape life and seek alcohol. So did the pathetic pleading of the overused "I'm so sorry" line. I loved her so much and felt deep *shame*, not just guilt, for the fear and sorrow I caused her, let alone my unreasonable expectation for her to forget my unjustifiable behaviors. I often pleaded that I wanted to spend my life with her, but my actions didn't match.

Alcohol and other substance addiction affect spouses, children, other family members, coworkers, and friends. It is truly a "family disease", which will be covered in more detail later in Volume II of this series.

Up to this point in my story, the primary negative consequences of my drinking were poor academics, financial waste, and relationship difficulties, but not enough pain for me to do much about it. In all this time, I was building an increasing tolerance to alcohol, needing more drinks to satisfy less. I was a prisoner of my own device.

The Treadmill Years

When our children started coming, four years after my college graduation, we had three beautiful babies in six years. I was rapidly increasing my responsibilities—at work and with coaching as well as those of our expanding young family. We also temporarily provided foster care for a little boy from the local children's home whom I met hanging around the gym at my school.

The growing personal and dual-career professional responsibilities heightened my stress and interfered with pleasure opportunities. Instead of playing sports myself, I devoted my downtime to coaching my own and other young kids on youth teams, and I also became involved in their other extracurricular school activities. I was not prepared to handle the stress of increasing responsibilities in all areas of my life, but I loved dancing with our little ones. We danced to Neil Diamond's September Morn and Heartlight, as well as Love Is The Answer by England Dan and John Ford Coley.

When I became assistant basketball coach at Denison University, my traveling throughout Ohio and neighboring states increased for purposes of recruiting, scouting, clinics, and camps. I was meeting other college and high school coaches around the region. With more auto travel at work and more air travel required of my main executive job, more opportunities to have a "few" drinks on the road presented themselves.

One summer while working the College of Wooster summer camp, I roomed with one of the new Indiana University assistant basketball coaches. We hit it off and became friends. He visited me in Newark when he was on the recruiting road in Ohio, and we stayed in touch frequently. He invited Bev and me several times to visit Bloomington, and we stayed with him, his wife, and their baby in their apartment.

I was able to observe firsthand the famous Indiana basketball coach Bob Knight and his staff (most became very successful college head coaches as well) conduct preseason practices. As a young coach, I learned a lot there. For those of you who are not into basketball, the Indiana teams in that era were Big Ten Conference and NCAA national champions, and Coach Knight was known as one of the best and most innovative coaches in the country for several decades. Sadly, he passed away recently.

I was excited when I got to accompany my friend when he picked up Coach Knight at the airport and took him home or directly to the field house. I went on a player evaluation trip by car with Coach Knight and several of his assistants to Nashville, Indiana. I can also remember being in Chicago on business and being invited by my friend to meet him and other Indiana staff for lunch. I was a lucky young coach to get to be up close with both Coach Hayes and then several Indiana University basketball staff members during my early coaching days.

In the mid '70s, after becoming the president/CEO of a new workforce development organization, and with my increasing coaching duties at the college level, I was on the road, moving from place to place. Out of town, I was in Chicago monthly, Washington, D.C. quarterly, and occasionally in other eastern US cities from Portland, Maine to New Orleans. My claim to fame was being on a panel on Cape Cod with Senator Ted Kennedy. Of course, I was loaded with liquid courage.

In Ohio, I was at meetings regularly in Columbus, Cleveland, Cincinnati, Portsmouth, and Akron-Canton. Then locally, I was in Newark, Delaware, Coshocton, Zanesville, and McConnellsville on an almost daily basis.

A growing executive job, larger coaching duties, a young and active family, and accepting newly elected and appointed state and national legislative responsibilities were the playing field for my workaholism, which often accompanies the "ism" of alcohol.

I was on a constant treadmill like a hamster on its spinning wheel. My sleep suffered. I could not seem to relax easily and felt considerable physical and mental tension. My escape was booze. Fight or flight was my reptilian brain's response because I had not yet developed the skills to manage life responsibly while minimizing fear and self-centered pride . . . and the drinking episodes. Whether it was neighborhood parties, golf, softball, coaching clinics, seminars, conferences, vacations, out of town flights, or local bars, I planned and seized upon any opportunity to feed the alcohol "monster" growing inside me, to binge drink into a numbness

At one point in my mid-twenties, I remember being so severely depressed I was suicidal and stayed awake for nearly an entire week without sleep. One of my AA sponsors later told me, "No wonder you were feeling depressed—you were constantly pouring large quantities of a depressant down your throat. How did you expect to feel?"

Not wishing to consider that alcohol and I were enmeshed as The Problem, I saw a psychiatrist to treat my depression and a few scary anxiety attacks. He suggested I go to group therapy to learn how to share my feelings and teach myself how to relax.

Oh, and he dared suggest I try a couple of glasses of wine before dinner to help me relax. Bingo! For me, this was a license to go fast forward. I enthusiastically followed the doctor's orders, but the couple of glasses of wine became a couple of bottles, before and after dinner. I made the mistake many other individuals with substance use disorders often try. I went to a therapist or counselor first instead of initially getting addiction-trained medical doctors and chemical-dependency counselors to help me.

Knowing what I know now, I realize medically assessing and addressing the physical symptoms of the disease first, reducing the "brain fog", significantly increases the chances of recovery and allows for much improved results from therapy, if needed.

Recalling my religious upbringing, I tried an increasing involvement at church and a men's group there. Both were beneficial, but they were not really equipped to identify or address my actual physical disorder related to alcohol.

I was clearly aware I had committed plenty of sins, as Granny had defined them early on for me, but I didn't understand how many wrongs or negative consequences were connected directly to my pride, my insecurities, and the predictable coping mechanisms of a substance use disorder with its dysfunctional brain physiology. I had an undiagnosed, progressive brain disease! Psychological thought with counseling was only effective later in the initial sobriety process, after the brain had cleared out the cobwebs.

All my therapy or church activities were not enough. The "fog" in my brain chemistry and the substance craving needed to subside before the words of recovery could sink in. That is why we insist "you cannot just think your way out of a chronic brain and body disease!"

The initial pit stop in auto racing has professional mechanics. A person struggling with substance misuse needs to see a doctor specifically trained in addiction screening, assessment and referral to treatment. This entry point of care necessitates a reliable screening, initial identification and brief intervention, a discussion of patient options, and a full-fledged assessment before any appropriate treatment assessment, diagnosis, and initial care plan is developed. The exception to this process would be immediate referral for acute patients to emergency care and likely subsequent withdrawal management care (formerly referred to as detoxification).

After my unsuccessful attempts at "controlling" my own drinking through counseling and church, plus not being screened by my family doctor for substance disease indicators, I sought out the father of an old high school buddy. This man had established himself as a local, well-known, recovering alcoholic and addiction medicine advocate. He was instrumental in establishing the first employee assistance program at the largest employer in our area.

Bob S., my first sponsor in recovery, introduced me to the disease model of alcoholism and the AA twelve-step recovery program. Quite surprisingly to me when I attended my first meetings, I ran into several of my own organization's board members. There were also other well-respected acquaintances who were "in the rooms" of AA when I first attended back then.

I received preliminary knowledge of the AA program in the four or five months I attended meetings (this is, unfortunately, an average stay for a program newcomer), so much so that I became sorely mistaken. I was convinced that I had basically figured out my problem. What I did not understand then was, in actuality, what I was seeking then was to learn a dependable way to "control" my drinking. I didn't see that it was the first drink that was always the initiator of my pain and adverse consequences. I didn't recognize the power alcohol actually exerted on me, all starting with the first drink.

I knew I had "a problem" with drinking but I just wasn't accepting I was a real "alcoholic." I fooled myself on purpose. I still could, in my clouded mind, lie to myself. As we say in recovery, "I compared out!". I wasn't in as bad of shape as some other heavy drinkers.

In my own misguided estimation, however dysfunctional I could be, I hadn't drank to the extent that "other folks I knew" had. Luckily, I had not lost my wife, family, job, money, or much of anything, so I thought. I had never been arrested, and I felt so much better physically after several months of not drinking anything. Shortly after arriving at my erroneous conclusion and attempting to rely on increased church involvement, I decided I would be able to drink sparingly and responsibly—only when and where it was acceptable, and in a very limited manner.

How long did that work?

The program of AA tells us that if we are not truly ready to stop drinking entirely on a daily basis (one day at a time), we should go back "out" into the world without the benefit and support of the recovery program and work on furthering our "lead," otherwise known as our "story," we share about ourselves in AA lead meetings. Becoming educated about the nature of this chronic disease is urged before going much further than this point.

They also tell you if you drink again, it won't be as enjoyable as you remembered it to be. That is exactly what I did! And they were exactly right! I was warned that alcohol use disorder is progressive, chronic, incurable, and increasingly damaging. Fantasy got the best of me.

After a while, your memory subconsciously tells you how chilling it will feel or how stress-relieving it will be to get high, but the reality of further drinking experiences never measures up to your anticipated illusions of euphoria or relaxation. It never gets better when you relapse or "go back out." The slide always gets steeper after a few drinking episodes following an abstinence period. The elevator is going down, never up! The consequences of the drinking pile up, while the cycle of withdrawal symptoms and cravings is exacerbated.

It was twenty-four more years of drinking heavily, especially binging, before I felt relief from the progressive pains of the illness. Alcoholism sneaks up on you. Judith Grisel labels it as the "sledgehammer" drug that keeps slamming you over the years.[18] Slow death! Almost unnoticeable at first. Certainly, a "cunning, baffling, and powerful" force of destruction, according to AA literature.[19]

The hamster monster (me) was racing increasingly faster on the spinning wheel of life. The CEO of an organization, a state- and federal-level policy activist, a college and high school basketball coach, a dad, a husband, a community volunteer, and an active church member, yet I could not satisfy the "hole in my soul." I could not live fast enough, work hard enough, accomplish enough, help enough people, perform well enough, or of course, drink enough, to satisfy my ego and pride in order to relieve the pain and suffering I felt inside and caused others when I drank.

Like most chronic progressive diseases, alcohol or drug addiction adversely alters the normal family structure into a group with dysfunctional behaviors. With this "family disease," members find different escape mechanisms or rationalized roles to cope with the chaos of living with unpredictability, irritability, chaos, and sometimes, downright fear.

The roles adopted by family members include the "enabler," "the hero child," "the silent one," "the rebel," "the controller," and other unconsciously developing behavioral personas. Did you realize that almost anyone closely or directly connected with the behavior of a sick alcohol or drug user is also likely to get sick themselves to some degree?

The relationship with my wife suffered the most episodic of disconnects. She and I both tried so many fruitless tactics to limit or control my drinking. In the long run, the disappointing efforts caused more frustration, chaos, and more opportunities for me to use self-pity and self-centered fear to rationalize consuming more alcohol.

The Superman-Slob Syndrome

Step Four of the Twelve Steps and Twelve Traditions of Alcoholics Anonymous describes "the power driver" and "the depressive" as personality extremes of a person with an alcohol use disorder.[20] One of my counselors used the analogy of this as the "Superman-Slob" syndrome, a constantly conflicting and extreme dynamic of split or oppositional behavior. At times I felt I could be an elite leader, executive, or coach. At other times, I felt I was failing everyone, falling short.

The same went for my roles of husband and father and as a person. Top-flight Greg conflicted with totally absent Greg. Superman or Slob was me, no in-between, no balance. Full speed ahead or laying around depressed and full of anxiety. The problem was actually me and my habits, the way I was thinking and responding to life. Alcohol was my solution.

My intense desire to succeed manifested itself in perfectionism and as a driven workaholic, often the case with individuals with alcohol or other substance use disorders. We think if we work hard enough, we project that we might be psychologically acceptable.

The stress, fear, and excess drinking created physical and mental exhaustion with periodic depression and its accompanying isolation. I was torn apart in both my public and private existence. As Judith Grisel so aptly titled her book *Never Enough*, I would suggest it appropriate to add a second relevant phrase to the title of her book. The full title I felt was "Never Enough, Never Good Enough."

In both my careers as an organizational leader and a basketball coach, I never felt competent enough or was working hard enough to be acceptable to myself or others. Our organization's performance, measured by federal standards, was, for twenty-three consecutive years, in the top one percent of nearly 700 similar organizations nationally. We had excellent measurable results, a supportive and politically nonpartisan board, and a clean financial record, yet I was never satisfied. I was certain my real lack of leadership capacity would be eventually exposed. I was fearful the respect I was seeking would be lost if people found out I wasn't Superman, but really a Slob. A Slob that hides in booze.

In basketball coaching, most of my teams were successful, but I couldn't accept losing. It now seems a perfectionists' illusion for me to think all losses were because I didn't coach well enough, prepare enough, focus enough, or make the appropriate decisions. But this unrealistic expectation of myself kept the bottle open.

I remember receiving a call one evening at the end of a season from Jim, a local sports editor. He was so excited. He told me he had, to my surprise, been behind an informal effort among his peers around Ohio to promote me for an Associated Press Ohio Basketball Coach of the Year award. He was calling to tell me I had won this designation. He was so proud of himself, and I truly think he thought I deserved the recognition.

Unfortunately, his call came shortly after my top-rated team had been upset in a tournament game by a team who had never beaten us before. Imagine a perfectionist's reaction to hearing about some external press accolade for coaching when I was convinced it was my coaching miscues that let down my own team. What a terrific group of great young men I was privileged to coach every day, and I had clearly failed them! No way was I going to accept a stupid award. I was ashamed! Once again I "drank Scotch whiskey all night long".

Well, apparently the award was already announced, and I had no choice but to act humble and appreciative. Inside, at that particular moment, it made me sick, disgusted, nauseated! What did the Superman-Slob split persona inside me choose to do with this dilemma of emotional shame? Of course, I pitifully drank myself into a lonely stupor. I wallowed in the self-generated stress of my own unreasonable expectations, highlighting my obvious imperfections and arrogantly refusing to acknowledge any other influence of control on the game.

There's a huge difference in wanting to learn from your mistakes and improve what you do—and beating yourself up emotionally for being a vulnerable perfectionist. At that time in my life, drinking was the only option I could see, the only route to escape the punishing failure of my unreasonable expectations.

At this point, my drinking was of the binge variety, but heavier and more frequently. I was exhibiting more noticeable outward signs of being intoxicated, like slurring my words, losing my balance, and unknowingly blacking out when intoxicated.

My wife knew I was in trouble long before I did. The consequences of my drinking were multiplying. Two major aspects of my life, two big leadership passions to which I devoted most of my adult life were, at this point, beginning to crumble inside my mind and confused dysfunctional thought processes.

My attitude toward life soured. I no longer wanted to be a part of steering the organization in what was becoming a growing partisan political climate. Nor was I interested in further coaching in an upper-class community with different values than me. Poor me, poor me, pour me a drink. Go away people and go away world! I've had enough of you. You are disturbing my sanity, and I don't need the hassle anymore.

I told myself I'd be perfectly content golfing, and, of course, enjoying myself, relaxing and drinking whenever I wished! Fight or flight response! By fleeing responsibility, I can finally escape all the stress . . . so I thought! Might not even need to drink so much!

THE WITHDRAWAL/NEGATIVE AFFECT STAGE

The "Functional" Alcoholic

No one, except my wife, knew the extent to which I had a "drinking issue." Only my youngest child ever had any suspicion of the extent of my problem. The last to leave home, she observed more of my disease behavior than the older two away at college.

There were three pivotal areas of responsibility that drove my life back then. The first was family, and I was active and involved in each of my kids' lives. The second was being the CEO of a large five-county workforce development agency. The third was coaching basketball, which was my original passion. As a workaholic, I drank when gaps in my responsibilities permitted. I sought and planned opportunities to drink.

In all my endeavors I appeared outwardly successful. My marriage, while having periodic difficulties due largely to my drinking, survived and appeared solid. Our three kids were all great, well behaved, and outstanding students, involved in extracurricular activities and sports. Eventually, each graduated from college, became very successful in their respective professions, and established beautiful families of their own.

At work, the local organization I was with was considered one of the better employment training entities in the country. It was more than a full-time job. Fortunately, early on, I knew as a coach that you are only as good as your players, and I was blessed to have a great, highly productive and dedicated staff across multiple counties for twenty-three years.

In conjunction with that job, I became immersed at the state, regional, and national level with legislative policy development that enhanced our local efforts. As an organizational leader and a head basketball coach, I appeared, my teams appeared, to be riding high. We were the champions, but it was no bed of roses.

Outwardly, I seemed a picture of success in my job and had a favorable reputation in both leadership fields, garnering a number of group and individual awards and accolades in each endeavor.

Inwardly, I intensely feared heights literally and figuratively. I traveled and flew a lot. To fortify myself, so I could board an aircraft, I would get a buzz on before I got to the airport. Of course, an obvious advantage of any out-of-town travel was…yes, the opportunity for unsupervised drinking.

This routine of get high, fly, remain high, fly home, lasted for several years, but I began experiencing severe hangovers, blackouts, and extreme exhaustion when I returned home. It was the beginning of my severe withdrawals and a long period of what I call feeling "yuk," intense irritability and negative emotions.

With time, this out-of-town flying routine changed. Not only did I need to get intoxicated before departure, but I also needed an extra travel day going and returning from my destination so I could recover in my hotel, sober up to do business, then get high again for the return flight home. Then when I got home, I needed time to sober up before I could function appropriately again. It was lonely out in space.

My drunken flights were often a sad comedy in themselves. Once I blacked out enroute to Chicago, landed, missed the departure, and landed in Milwaukee. Where was the flight crew when I needed them? Not my fault!

I had a habit on my drunken flights of pretending to be another person in conversations with other passengers. On one trip to Chicago one morning, I sat next to a big guy and we began talking about Coach Hayes, my idol. Woody had just been fired because during a bowl game a Clemson player ran his helmet into Coach's fist (my version). I told this guy sitting next to me on the plane in no uncertain terms that if I had the chance, I would let the guy that fired Woody have a piece of my wrath.

Well, I discovered too abruptly I was talking to Hugh Hindman sitting next to me. Coach Hindman was the athletic director at Ohio State who unfortunately was given the order from above to fire Woody! Somehow, we landed at O'Hare without him stuffing my mouth with his foot. You would think I had learned my lesson, but no.

Another time in flight, I decided to impress this distinguished-looking, gray-haired man seated next to me. I decided to disguise myself as a CIA agent and introduced myself to him after takeoff and drinks were served:

> Distinguished Man: "And what do you do for a living, Mr. Webb?"
> Greg W: "Call me Roger. I uh, well, I work for, well, the government."
> Distinguished Man: "You do? Well, that's great, Roger. What department?"
> Greg W: "Sir, let's talk about something else. My job is classified!"
> Distinguished Man: "Classified! Well now you've gotten my curiosity up, Roger. You can tell me. I've been around the government."
> Greg W: "Oh well, sir, I uh, I work for the ugh 'company.' You know."
> Distinguished Man: "By company, do you mean what I think you mean?"
> Greg W: "Yes, sir, the agency, but they require my confidentiality."
> Distinguished Man: "I know, you're right, Roger! I work for the government too! Where is your office, Roger?"
> (I pondered his inquiry briefly, then blurted out a foolish response)
> Greg W: "D.C., sir, the Executive Office Building (EOB) next to the White House is my station right now."
> Distinguished Man: "Wow! My office is also in the EOB as well. You'll have to visit me. What a coincidence! What floor is your office on?"
> Greg W: Well, his question stunned me! I couldn't remember how many floors constituted that building. Curiously, slowly I stammered, "Uh . . . May I ask your name, sir?"
> Distinguished Man: "Yes, young man. I'm Alex, Alex Haig."

Oh my God! Then I realized! I was actually speaking to General Alexander Haig, the Secretary of State under President Reagan. It's a wonder he didn't have me jailed, or "institutionalized" for impersonating a federal officer. Oh well, another bullet grazed my intoxicated flight illusions! I barely dodged another disaster.

This travel routine became part of my flying "life on the treadmill." I looked for mental and physical escape from stress. There was coaching with which I was passionately obsessed. Come to think of it, my life was a huge obsession to succeed, to be good enough.

I spent twenty plus years coaching college and high school basketball teams. Most seasons our teams were very successful, winning around 80 percent of our games due to my good fortune to have the talented and dedicated kids I coached and the assistant coaches who worked with me.

External perceptions can be deceiving. In my case, outwardly I was functional. Inside I was stressed, almost always in some emotional turmoil, always scurrying from one place to another, trying my best to demonstrate I was competitive, competent, and in control.

I was indeed blessed but was so fearful of failure. Ironically, the disease of alcohol use disorder was knocking me off any pedestal I was driven to reach.

TORN IN HALF/FEELING LIKE "YUK"

Constantly in the rush-rush lifestyle, I was in search mode, planning for opportunities to escape the grind. My refuge, my best friend, was the "isolator," the "rapacious creditor": alcohol! Cookouts, parties, conferences, golf, weekends, going out to dinner. I was eager to find that moment when I could drink my angst away.

After my binges, I had terrific hangovers that would keep me in bed for at least a day. I suffered from withdrawals and was often in some state of pain, physical and emotional. Of course, I was irritable and discontent and "didn't know why." It was a vicious cycle: drink heavily and slowly revive just enough to find the next drink and a brief sense of relief.

When I got to this point, my cycle of needing to drink and experiencing withdrawals was in control of my life, and I couldn't escape from that prison. I often felt the guilt of drinking and the shame of not being able to stop or control it. No matter how many times I intended to, promised to quit, there were enough reasons "poor-me" needed that drink. I was captured and began drinking without much forethought.

Up in the morning, feeling like crap, swearing off booze for that day, and then by midday I was planning my next drink. I was in what I now understand as the "anticipation/preoccupation" stage of planning and "craving" the drink, a common phenomenon of addiction and surefire indicator of later-stage disease or severe alcohol use disorder.

Luckily, I had so far escaped the often-apparent outward consequences of this disease stage. Although I was arrested once for DUI, somehow the case was able to be dismissed because the Breathalyzer malfunctioned.

I was never incarcerated; the damages done to this "functional alcoholic" were mostly hidden. I suffered consequences in the relationship with my wife, mostly the result of my self-centeredness, never being satisfied, wanting to be "right," and being frightened of my commitment to her. I knew she deserved better than my unpredictability and she would be completely justified in kicking me out . . . but she didn't! It was what recovery groups phrase as "God doing for me what I could not do for myself."

I am eternally grateful to her for her patience, forgiveness, and commitment to me, and her dedication to detachment from my disease, despite my self-centered fear of losing her.

THE ANGER MONSTER

I did not then know that anger is a serious behavioral by-product of an alcohol use disorder. I did realize I could get angry instantaneously. Even when I was a youngster, if I pitched a baseball game and we lost, my little league coach, a wonderful man, would find me alone in the dugout crying. He would console me, long after the rest of the team had gone home.

Before basketball games that I coached, I would pray to remain calm. My temper was unfortunately a negative part of my overall demeanor as a coach. I did everything I possibly knew to keep my anger at bay. It was like I had an "anger monster" inside me waiting for the opportune time to leap out.

The anger monster demonstrated how out of control my life really was. It was about not accepting life as it actually was, trying to maintain the self-illusion with an intense internal effort to control the outcomes of events, like basketball games. My instant anger expressed outwardly was the result of the internal fear of "not getting what I want" or "losing what I had."

Anger is a natural fear-driven human emotion. We all feel it. It's how we deal with it or recognize and manage it that matters. In alcohol or drug withdrawal, anger is a fuel like gasoline, just ready and waiting for a flame to ignite it.

Now that I understand more about alcohol withdrawal syndrome, I see how anger, irritability, and unmanageability are part of an addicted person's life. As Judith Grisel points out in her laws of psychopharmacology, all drugs either speed up or slow down the rate of what is already in the brain.

Alcohol does not cause anger. It expedites it! The withdrawal syndrome from the absence of alcohol use causes sufficient irritability and discontentment. The chemical combination of alcohol and the stress hormone cortisol can create a vicious cycle. A chemically induced monster can instantly appear at the slightest provocation!

I avoided drinking around players or before games in season, but I just recently realized an interesting point: On non-game days, I would be home and, at this stage of the disease, have drinks in the evening while I watched films or made out practice or game plans for the next day. But on game days or nights, I didn't have any drinks for a twenty-four- to forty-eight-hour period.

This lack of alcohol created acute withdrawal symptoms and resulted in considerable game-time irritability, the result of a diseased brain absent its chemical stress reliever. The negative consequences of not drinking during any high-stress times for me became a punishment. In my seemingly life-or-death coaching battles, the absence of alcohol physiologically triggered my brain to default to edgy fight-or-flight survival behaviors.

My self-described label for this time of my life is feeling like crap or "yuk" most of the time. The US Surgeon General and others have defined this emotional state of what I call "yuk" as the "negative affect." It involves a general feeling of dysphoria, anxiety, irritability, depression, and decreasing stress tolerance with corresponding increases in stress manifestations. Sleep, appetite, and nutrition are adversely affected.

A huge spiritual enemy, self-centered fear, becomes a front-and-center force in your brain during this "yuk" stage. Many who experience these symptoms become lifeless, confused, physically sick, and even paranoid. Many nights I would awaken around 3 a.m. and ruminate about the next day, rarely able to return to sleep. It was the night I feared the most.

In recovery, we identify being "hungry, angry, lonely, and tired" (HALT) as key danger signals that our lives are not in balance and our brains and body health need an immediate tune-up. All of these signals of HALT warn of potential harm to our well-being, triggers that cue us to drink or use other substances. These triggers are our enemies, our opponents. They are the reasons, the illusions, the lies we tell ourselves!

Alcohol and other substance addiction creates a psychological conflict known as "cognitive dissonance", emanating in several brain regions. In 1957, Leon Festinger introduced this term as "a state of conflicting beliefs or thoughts that creates an uncomfortable mental state." This discomfort is created when you are aware that your belief system and your behavior don't match. In simple terms, people with a substance use disorder eventually develop an internal mental dialogue between positive longer-term health choices and short-term gratification. These options are sometimes consciously made, but at many other times, they are made without conscious awareness. Unless our brain is retrained, almost always our internal choice, our habitual response is, "need relief now!"

THE PREOCCUPATION/ANTICIPATION STAGE

The Capture Point

When the cycle of withdrawals and a negative emotional state continues, the various regions of your brain can become more dysfunctional. Although chaos is occurring internally, with the world around us we continue to maintain the illusion that we are still in control of our lives. We deny reality! We are in denial! The river in Egypt! We are living the big lie, to ourselves and others. We blame and deny!

Without going into the deep detail of neurology, one part of your brain is the center of much of your thoughtful decision-making or your executive thinking center. It is called the *prefrontal cortex* region, the most recently advanced area of the brain in our human evolutionary development.

This part of the brain is asked to consider the option of taking a drink. And simply stated, the thoughtful, appropriate response is "no" or "not now" or any version of a conscious decline. The "thinking" cortex raises the inhibitive and negative consequences connected to "having a drink." Past memories are consulted. However, thoughtful consideration usually is overridden by instant gratification. By "default," the reptilian brain's (the *brain stem*'s) instinctive desire seeks quick relief.

Additionally, other parts of your brain also weigh into the question. Often these other brain responses are from damaged or overused, chemically imbalanced sources. Due to damages already incurred (in the brain's stress management, memory, reward, or other neurochemical systems), your confused, tired thinking yields to your survival instincts.

This quick "fight, flight, or freeze" response emanates from the survival center in the lower brain stem area. You may think, Hey, I am so stressed out or I'm hungry or angry or lonely or tired. And you'll think, I need—no, I deserve!—to get away, an escape for just a drink or so . . . Then off we go! We gotta survive and escape the pain!

The subconscious memories of our previous learning and the old memories of our previous experiences that recall pleasurable drinking experiences become unconscious deciders in the fight-or-flight decision to drink. The reptilian brain, in a sense, overrides thoughtfulness. The quicker, more expedient, happier-sounding solution promises some measure of relief to the silent suffering.

This is why alcoholics drink, even though we know it's not smart or logical. We are captured! Our brains aren't well. We need to, we have to, we decide to seek a substance for relief from our "yuk" and our stress-induced life.

After I got sober I heard an audio tape of California Supreme Court Justice Don Gates. I'll never forget his message. Judge Gates said "the only difference between a person with an alcoholic use disorder and a normal person is the phenomenon of 'craving,' the compulsion to drink in spite of predictable negative consequences and despite our best effort not to drink."

Technically his assessment is not totally accurate, but he made a very important point back then. Some individuals just have the genetic, physiological, or neurological differences that are factors allowing the disease to develop and progress more easily.

At this craving stage, we are usually no longer consciously making the decision to drink. It is made for us by dysfunctional neural pathways and chemical imbalances in our brains. Now we are drinking, fighting, and taking flight just to exist, to maintain. Unfortunately, the consequences of our drinking or using are accumulating rapidly, growing exponentially. We become emotionally, physically, and spiritually bankrupt.

Our single purpose at this stage of the disease is basic emotional and physical survival based upon the seeking and acquisition of the next fix. This is, in this severe stage of the disorder, our only existential anticipation, our overriding and most vital life consideration. When is our next available opportunity? At this point, we will lie, sneak, cheat, manipulate, and steal to set up the next drink or use. We constantly are chasing relief and our neurologically "craving" brain demands our full attention.

The failure to manage the growing stresses in life with a dysfunctional brain system combines with the spiraling losses of personal connections in life to create the perfect storm of fear and chaos. Our spirit is imprisoned. We are now neck-deep in the accumulated consequences of our behavior, and sadly immersed in the self-generated flood of rationalizations and defense mechanisms we use to justify our drinking or using behavior.

We pretend to be okay, even believe it is true. We still possess some sense of false pride that we are steering our own ship, even though our particular vessel is clearly sinking.

"Hey, I'm not that bad! I'm not like old 'so and so' who is a 'lush.'" "I'm actually doing better." "I'm not sick, I'm just stressed, tired of being falsely blamed and complained to or about. I work hard, provide for my family well, and am generally respected. What's the problem? I deserve to relax more."

"All I need is a little break, maybe a vacation or a move, a change (what recovery folks call the illusion of a geographical cure)". "If I change jobs (or hobbies or toys or houses), I'll be better off (feel better, be healthier.)" "Maybe buying a boat is what I need!"

My brain is now obviously captured. The overwhelmingly predominant urge is anticipating, attaining the drink or drug. The phenomenon of "craving" becomes continuous. The damage being done is cumulative—physical, mental, emotional, social, and spiritual.

My own physiological repercussions from years of drinking include quadruple heart bypass surgery, coronary artery disease, the installation of a pacemaker/defibrillator, cancer, the implant of a breathing stimulator in my neck, liver damage, migraine headaches, kidney disease, a necrotic gallbladder, digestive issues, and a recent heart failure diagnosis. That's just the known physical damage of my addiction. I have no idea if there is a relationship between my drinking and the two forms of cancer, for which I've been successfully treated.

In this craving stage of the disease, the imprisoned person, the silent sufferer, is so invested in the drink or drug that accessibility to it is planned and achieved at all costs. My retirement from my two careers freed up so much more time for me to pursue my obsession.

Clearly aware I was drinking excessively; I remained incapable of acknowledging that I needed help. I could see myself spiraling toward the basement floor, but the control panel was stuck and the door locked.

My increased free time and my need for "maintenance drinking" turned any freedom I had into my incarceration in the maximum-security prison of my mind. Oddly, I was both the prisoner and the jailer. I was locked up in "the bondage of self"

I lost my enthusiasm for both leading a company and coaching. I had surrendered my life to "the freedom" to drink when it suited me. In the immediate years of my retirement, I wandered into several new areas that were temporarily interesting. I consulted with both large and small businesses and agencies about team building, training, and organizational development. I served as the part-time youth director of the local Presbyterian Church, returned to coaching for a couple of years as an assistant, and spent a year or so as the interim director of a local mental health agency and a day center for developmentally disabled adults.

In conjunction with my stint at the church, I decided to attend classes at the Methodist Theological Seminary of Ohio. A longtime interest, I decided to study spiritual life, but not for purposes of ordination. Ironically, when I first enrolled in classes I was in the depths of my alcohol disease. Only later, after beginning sobriety, did I return and focus my attention at the seminary on addiction ministry.

Never would I have pictured my life as it was in the beginning days of attending the seminary. I was leading two separate lives. In the daytime, I would go to class, study, and write papers, and then daily in the late afternoon I would drink until I passed out at home. I knew there was something wrong with this picture, but I did not want other people to know my secret. I could not stop and knew inside I needed help.

THE BASEMENT FLOOR

The sun began to creep into the shadows under the freeway bridge that arched over North 21st Street in my hometown on that warm early August Sunday morning in 1999.

I remember that morning so vividly, even today. In desperation, I eased my car to the side of the road and parked under the bridge in the shade. It was quiet, almost void of traffic, well before church drivers were even out and about.

The time had arrived, I could no longer avoid facing my helplessness, the hopelessness I experienced with alcohol. A critical decision became evident in my mind, the impact of which would affect me and certainly my family forever.

Reclining in the driver's seat that tilted back in my Camaro, I was in a nearly horizontal position, my hands and body were shaking almost uncontrollably. Yet, eventually the critical choice crystallized in my mind. A stark reality appeared under the passenger seat, a silver weapon that was within reach and could instantly end my suffering.

Earlier that summer, my wife and I were sitting on our back deck near dusk. Typically, I was drinking martinis to enable me to sink into my nightly oblivion when the front doorbell rang. An older lady at the door said she was from the Athens, Ohio AA group and brought a young lady with her who needed our help. At first unrecognizable due to her weight loss, it took my wife and me several moments to actually realize the girl who needed help was our daughter, a college junior. Fortunately, she admitted to us she needed help.

After several frantic phone calls, we were advised to take her to Shepherd Hill, a treatment center for substance addiction, fortunately nearby in our hometown. She was professionally assessed, diagnosed, and admitted there quickly. She remained there for several months, the best decision we ever made.

Unable to visit her for several weeks, my first opportunity to see her came early one Sunday morning when she and other treatment patients were having breakfast in the nearby hospital cafeteria. I walked into there, wreaking of alcohol from a previous night's binge. As I leaned over to kiss my daughter hello, she said "Dad what are you doing, coming in here smelling like alcohol? Don't you understand all of us here are trying to stay alive, and you are not helping us at all! Please don't come back like that!"

The shame I felt was enormous, unbearable. Embarrassed and in tears, I ran through the exit into the hospital parking lot, jumped into my car, and began driving aimlessly around town with nowhere to go, nowhere to hide from myself. I turned onto North 21st Street and felt as though I could not drive any further, so I pulled off onto the berm under the expressway bridge.

With no traffic in sight, I turned off the motor and laid back thinking about my drinking past and how it developed into the present helplessness. Weakened by its effects, I scolded myself for not even being in a state to help my daughter when she needed me. My life was chaos, confusion, loneliness, shame, anger, and emptiness. My body actually shook with fear.

I could no longer redirect blame for my anxieties and stresses elsewhere. I was the problem! It was me who poured the booze down my throat! I was lost, and not the person I really wanted to be inside.

Saint Augustine said, "If you really want to know a person, don't ask them what they think or what they believe in, ask them what they truly love." God forgive me, I loved alcohol! It had been my best friend, my mistress, my escape hatch. It had allowed me to take liberties with my behaviors and to deflect both my actions and my cares.

As I laid back in the car seat, I could see that my whole world had shriveled up into the sole pursuit of the drink. It had been a long time since I got a euphoric feeling from its use. My tolerance for the drug was no longer increasing. On the contrary, with two or three stiff drinks now I was passing out. Then, in the later stage of my disease, I was awakening from my stupors feeling like "the bottom of a birdcage." I was craving, but receiving no pleasure, only punishment.

As I finally considered my options in the car that Sunday, I considered applying a permanent, instant solution to my suffering and reflected on what impact that would have on my wife and family. I thought about what kind of example I would be setting for my children and all the former players I loved, if I just quit life. Lines from a familiar song by Kenny Loggins kept running through my head. ("This is it, make no mistake where you are / You're going no further, until it's over and done.")

For some reason, my right hand reached for my flip phone. Shaking, I could barely hold it still enough to find and dial the number of a friend who I knew was in the AA program. This friend, with whom I used to play poker and drink, had said to me a few months previously, "Coach, we are waiting for you." I knew what he meant about "having an open chair" for me at local AA meetings. Fortunately, I recalled his invitation that morning of my desperation.

The recovery community speaks of this type of experience as a "Higher Power" thing and would label it as God doing for me what I could not do for myself. In my experience, this axiom is a substantiated truth of the spiritual gift of grace. In this instance it was lifesaving and eventually life restoring. My elevator had hit the basement, and the heavy door I thought had already closed and locked was sprung open! If I lost my faith in you, there would be nothing left of me.

THE TERMS OF SURRENDER

My friend and I had a late coffee that morning and went together to an AA meeting that evening. That day, August 1, 1999, the day I sat in my car ashamed and contemplating suicide, was also the day "someone reached out the hand of recovery" to me. It was the birth of a reboot, a restart, a restoration of my life. That day, I was finally open to and received help! And I found hope!

I surrendered to the disease that week and finally admitted I lacked any power when it came to alcohol use. My life had become unmanageable because of my uncontrollable use of booze.

For me, surrendering to my own powerlessness was the first step in liberation. This was the day "the jailer was sent home so the prisoner could be freed." There was hope! A way out! Others had found it, one day at a time, and with help I could too. And I wanted that freedom. Freedom, you know, is the opposite of addiction.

I knew I was no longer alone. These people in the recovery program knew me, knew exactly what I was experiencing. Regardless of many other individual differences, we all had one thing in common: the desire to stop drinking or using drugs. I was one of them! They laughed a lot, I belonged, and as one old timer often described such an orientation, "they were good to me"!

I remember a couple of lines from an inspiring verse one of my seminary professors shared with us in class. It gave me hope and placed my own recovery into the spiritual realm. If I remember correctly his words were from a lesser known Stevie Wonder song. "Lonely one of young so broken-hearted / Traveling down the rigid road of life / Using pharmaceutical extractions to find Paradise." If you are struggling I suggest you listen to "YOU WILL KNOW."

THE GIFT OF RECOVERY ACCEPTED

The Climb Out

Early sobriety was not easy. My brain craved alcohol for quite some time, and my body went through withdrawal without it. I could not have become or maintained being sober alone. Ironically, almost everyone I've ever known to want recovery fools themselves first by asserting, "I can do it myself!" This is the lie you tell yourself, so you don't have to be responsible to any "recovery teammates."

Each day I ate breakfast with other guys in the recovery community and went to meetings with them. Dave, one of those old breakfast mates in recovery, liked to say, "they were good to me," referring to the experienced recovery members who take you under their wings when you arrive.

Truly, it was recovery "one day at a time" with considerable effort and support to deal with my continuing craving and withdrawal pains, which remained in early abstinence, but eventually cleared over time. It was the period of time for a simultaneous beginning of new life for both my daughter and me, as well as for my wife in Al-Anon. she was our heart light.

I was wrapped in a blanket of experience, support, knowledge, and care by the local recovery community. Day by day, my life got better. My craving dissipated over time, and I am eternally grateful for their love and teaching and friendship. It really was a team that carried me. I was the rookie. Today they still carry me forward, and now I am an active, experienced member of the largest team on the planet—two million members and counting! These groups light up the world and set us free.

The Plug in the Jug

Early in recovery, the team helped me to avoid drinking on a daily basis. The more difficult part (I had stopped drinking thousands of times) was "staying stopped." It is so easy to relapse. When you start feeling good or feeling bad or feeling confident or feeling lonely or for that matter, feeling anything, it takes very little emotional pull in early sobriety to convince you that "one drink won't hurt."

Our saying for that rationalization is "one drink is too many, a thousand is not enough." It is the first drink that makes the big difference, and we have to learn how to avoid it at all costs.

The recovery community has developed a lot of little sayings or phrases that you hear in early sobriety that are intended to help promote serenity and prevent relapse. You constantly hear "one day at a time," "easy does it," "hope is found here," "first things first," "keep it simple," "don't overthink it," "be grateful for what you have," "do the next right thing," and many other brief slogans that have a habit of being recalled in your brain just at that critical moment when you need a positive direction in a real-life situation.

When I told my recovery community I was ashamed and felt guilty for things I did, they comforted me with one of those little slogans. They said "you are not a bad person trying to get good. You are a sick person trying to get well." It took a while to comprehend, assimilate, and then accept my disease and accept from where and how my unwanted behaviors (what AA labels "character defects") emanated.

By the way, addicted people are not special in regard to harmful behavior or negative attributes. All humans belong to this club. The major difference is for someone like me, I am grateful to have asked for and been given unconditional access to the most satisfying lifelong, personal development and coaching program that is available daily anywhere around the world—and it is tuition free for anyone who has the desire to attend! Be forewarned though: You may end up making the coffee! You also might find your ability to drink alcohol or use drugs now spoiled by what you learn.

Promises Made, Promises Kept

After I was in recovery for a while and the urges to drink began to lessen, I learned that I was not just "staying stopped," but I was being taught "how to live life on life's terms." Rather than maintaining high expectations and attempting to control life and the behavior of others, I was learning acceptance of what actually is. They told me to focus on the work, the process, and to forget about the outcomes!

From recovery, I have learned that the only control I really have is over myself—my own mindset, behaviors, and responses to life. Taking the pressure off myself to be in control of things I cannot manage has dialed down my stress level and that of others around me as well.

I underwent a transformation at the hands of the recovery community. I am learning how to accept myself as a vulnerable human being (not either of the extremes of superman or slob). I am being taught how I could respond differently to life and its stresses, and how to handle responsibility without unreasonable standards of perfection. They showed me how to accept my mistakes, forgive myself, do the necessary leg work to change, and let the results take care of themselves.

I admitted responsibility for my own actions, and I admitted my powerlessness over other people, places, and things in my life. One of my recovery sponsors says it's all about "getting right-sized," which he equates to the essence of humility. Amazing grace!

I have, over time, become aware of the recovery goal of learning to "live life on life's terms." It is a new lifestyle based upon the fundamental and universal spiritual principles of surrender of will, acceptance of reality, the humility to know how I fit in the whole picture of life, and an individual spiritual path that seeks positive relationships with myself, other human beings, and a loving divinity.

By following this new lifestyle of recovery, maintaining total abstinence from alcohol or other addictive drugs, the stresses in my life have lessened considerably. Many positive results are naturally occurring in my life because I am better at "pausing" before I respond to people and events. I try to carefully pick the energizing "people, places, and things" in my life and avoid those that drain my energy.

By seeking serenity, courage, and a little wisdom, I am trusting my own instincts and my own navigation of life with help and without resorting to the illusionary reinforcement of alcohol. I realize I don't have to solve everything. In fact, very little is in my control. My wife taught me about FOG— fear, obligation, guilt—and she advised me not to use any of those as justification for my actions. Great advice!

I don't have as many problems, personal or financial, when I am not drinking. Some of my problems were from pride and fears of reality that never actually developed like I projected in my mind. My fears and anxieties have been able to be "shared and halved" with close friends and mentors in recovery.

The recovery community teaches that "fear faced fades." I shared problems of mine with others, released them into the universe, or what recovery refers to as "a higher power." I consider a "higher power" as including your own understanding of your supreme being and also including anyone who knows more than you about a particular area. An example is if you have a toothache, a dentist is a "higher power" you call on for help. Interdependence, not independence, is key to recovery.

Now more peaceful and fulfilled, the natural reward system in my brain has been restored enough for me to notice and enjoy the natural beauty, gifts, and joys of life, both external and internal. Relationships with and the service of others have restored purpose to my life.

Despite the overwhelming upturn in my quality of life during sobriety, I still have self-centered issues. I try to work on them and evaluate my progress each night. I conduct a daily inventory of the instances of when I display my pride, ego, judgment, lust, anger, instant competitive responses, or an appetite for more than I really need.

It seems nearly every night in my daily mental and spiritual wrap-up something appears in my brain that occurred that day to remind me that one or more of my issues has resurfaced and needs my attention. Now I know where to get help and support, from my own higher powers of recovery.

Since I have been a perfectionist, I am sure these issues are lessons reminding me of "being right-sized," just being human. In Hebrew, the root meaning of the word *perfect* did not refer to being mistake free. "Perfect" meant "being honed by the fire of God." In other words, it was not referring to what a person did for themselves, but instead what was being done to mold or sculpture them into a healthier person.

William James, in his classic <u>Varieties of Religious Experiences</u> described these "spiritual awakenings" as much more apt to occur through the influences of other human beings and normal worldly experiences, than in spectacular epiphanies like St. Paul had on the road to Damascus with the burning bush.[21]

My friend Ben R. often says, "I am not the man I was, I am not the man I want to be, and I am not the man I'm going to be." If I don't drink, and I continue to let others help me, and I serve others, then I have a great chance of having this promise come true as well. I am so grateful I have had the wonderful experience of being an alcoholic and practicing recovery, one day at a time.

I would be remiss if I didn't point out the role my wife of fifty-seven years has played. She has been so supportive of both our daughter and me from the beginning of our recovery journeys. She has been actively involved in Al-Anon support groups since 1999. Without her new knowledge, love, patience, support, forgiveness, and active involvement in the recovery program, I am certain my recovery would have been so much more difficult. I am also certain my daughter feels the same way.

Perhaps the greatest gift to me in sobriety is gratitude for what I have had, much of what I took for granted before experiencing enough recovery to appreciate my greatest blessings, not the least of which was my loving wife. Nobody does it better.

THE GAME: COACH'S STORY

Several years ago, Bev and I decided to make a fall trip to Deep Creek, Maryland, a beautiful and secluded resort area, where we renewed our marriage vows. The memory of this trip comforts me now. We each wrote and then recited new vows to each other as we held each other on a hidden shore of that peaceful lake. We danced to our song, Neil Young's Harvest Moon, as the sunset glittered across the shimmering water.

No, I didn't begin my life desiring to be addicted to or possessed by alcohol. I wasn't taught to take life and all I was given for granted. My love for life and the people in it were slowly replaced by my love for a mind-altering substance. It happened to me over time. I was unaware I was predisposed genetically or that my childhood trauma of separation and a sequestered environment could have played a role in its manifestation.

We are all wired differently and have different life experiences. Some of us have a genetic and physiological susceptibility to experience alcohol or drug addiction, or a combination of both. My daughter continues to be such an inspiration to me. She and I are the very lucky ones to have received and accepted help before it was too late. She found recovery in her early twenties, I at age fifty-four.

In many ways—and you hear many of us recovering folks say this—I am truly grateful to have an alcohol use disorder and am blessed to have experienced recovery up to now. How else would I have learned to stop drinking, stay stopped, to live life on life's terms, and to experience life as "happy, joyous, and free" most of the time.

Thank you, recovery team and teammates, for coaching me and always being there for me! You have snatched me from the jaws of defeat and led me to the thrills of victory—up to today! I pray I never lose awareness of how powerful my opponent of addiction is, a beast scheming for my next entrapment. I know today I don't have to engage the enemy if I maintain relearning, practice my fundamental skills daily, live by the principles my recovery coaches have taught me, and hang with my recovery community teammates. And above all else, I cannot have the first drink, anytime, anywhere! Forgetaboutit!

"More, Broader, Kinder, Earlier, Faster, Better, Longer!"

SCOUTING THE OPPONENT:
ALCOHOL AND OTHER SUBSTANCE USE DISORDERS

"MODERN MEDICAL DISEASE MODEL" OF SUBSTANCE USE DISORDER (SUD)

"When the jailer goes home, the prisoner is freed."

Neurological research has overwhelmingly determined that addiction to alcohol and other mind-altering substances is a medical disease that clearly and adversely impacts the brain and body. Most medical organizations and addiction experts adhere to this "modern medical disease model" as the base starting point for the screening, assessment, diagnosis, and treatment of substance addiction.

Officially labeled as the substance use disorder spectrum (SUD), with a "mild" to "moderate" to a "severe" diagnosis, the disease is scientifically considered a primary, progressive, chronic, and prematurely fatal (if untreated) physiological disorder. The brain/body dysfunction, the neurological disorder of SUD, does however have significant physical, behavioral, social, and spiritual ramifications.

We no longer view substance addiction as a subset of another mental health disorder or psychological condition. The intrinsic biological nature of disease is impacted largely by genetic predisposition, environment, culture, familial connections, trauma, concurrent mental health issues, and other influencing factors, such as the availability of substances and the age of onset (earliest use of alcohol or other addictive drug).

Here is an important distinction to keep in mind. Substance disorder or disease is not a mental health issue in itself and needs initial primary physical care. Substance use disorders are separate from mental health diagnoses. People with mental health issues can develop substance use disorders. Individuals with substance use issues can also have a co-occurring substance use disorder. And those with addiction disease almost always experience results of physical, neurological, psychological, mental, emotional, social, and spiritual dysfunction.

The idea that having a substance use disorder should be treated initially as a psychological problem is misleading and frequently diagnosed inappropriately by rehabs to potentially gain more financially from their fee structures. *Physical* conditions should be treated by *physicians* first!

Contrary to the outworn and stigmatizing misconception of addiction being a result of moral absence or a personality disorder, addiction has multiple risk factors (genetics and environment being the largest ones); however, both the causes and the effects are rooted in the anatomy and physiology of the brain, the rest of the central nervous system, and the body organs and systems.

Next to genetic predisposition, environmental factors have been linked to the increased susceptibility of young people to develop addictions. What we traditionally think of in examining environmental factors is often the issue of abuse, and the word "abuse" conjures up physical maltreatment in most of our minds.

Obviously, physical abuse in childhood can and does create long-term psychological consequences of trauma for many individuals, as does sexual abuse. These abuses definitely create increased odds of people developing all kinds of issues, substance addiction included.

However, what often goes unnoticed or overlooked in addiction risk factors is emotional trauma. There again, with emotional trauma, we tend to perceive it most often as a perpetration of aggressive language. What I have become familiar with later in the scientific study of my personal addiction risk factors is a different kind of childhood trauma. I am now quite certain that I experienced several unintentional traumatic experiences as a child that, as well as my genetics, contributed to my increased risk of developing an alcohol use disorder. I will elaborate on my experiences and some science that corroborates my "unintentional trauma."

I am not suggesting emotional issues need treatment first for people with substance use disorders. Sufficiently clearing the brain of chemical dysfunction and treating the physiological symptoms is, in my view, initially essential to then proceed with counseling or therapy.

A BASIC PATTERN OF ALL MIND-ALTERING SUBSTANCES IN THE BRAIN

This is an important, essential point of our writing! No matter what drug or drugs are involved, whether legal or illegal; whether medically prescribed or obtained on the street; the process of all drugs entering the brain follows a similar and, up to a point, predictable pattern. (1) Every mind-altering drug causes specific initial effects. (2) All drugs cause the brain to respond with a countermeasure, or adaptation. (3) With continued use, all mind-altering substances eventually cause brain/organ damage and dysfunction.

Also significant, research has indicated many individuals who eventually become addicted are born with or have anatomical, chemical, and physiological brain/body differences or abnormalities before they ever drink or use, or before they are born, for that matter. Genetics, epigenetics, prenatal and postnatal conditions and care, and other uncontrollable physiological elements leave some people more susceptible, or neurologically "sensitive," to addictive substances.

So if you are not addicted to or abusing alcohol or drugs, be grateful you weren't either anatomically and physiologically susceptible at birth, or you avoided the other environmental risk factors in your life that can activate the disorder. And, because of your luck at birth, you can drop the pretense that it was all your own outstanding behavioral choices that separate you from people with addictions. Who knows, you may be addicted to yourself!

Like many people, including my dad, me, and my daughter, we had no clue that beginning at birth our odds of genetic addiction risk were four times higher than the norm. Like an overwhelming percentage of Americans, we each began to experiment with alcohol and initially drank recreationally or socially. At that point of our "onset" of drinking, we clearly chose to drink! And the responsibility for that initial decision rested with us at that stage.

Unaware we were predisposed genetically to addiction, with continued drinking, we began to have consequences. Eventually our experimental use progressed to binge drinking and then more consequental intake (heavy drinking) that led us along the spectrum of a substance use disorder.

US DRINKING CHARACTERISTICS

Various sources indicate that approximately 12 to 20 percent or more of adults who drink alcohol, our disease progresses to a moderate or severe disorder. Surprisingly, nearly one third of all US adults don't drink any alcohol at all! Equally significant, up to 40 percent of Americans who drink alcohol experience enough negative consequences from drinking to meet the criteria for misuse or a mild level of an alcohol use disorder.

Those in my family who activated a substance use disorder began to drink at different ages, on our own different timetables. Females and seniors tend to progress more quickly with varied patterns of use. We all eventually experienced a mild, then moderate, then severe state of progressive substance disorder. At different ages of life ranging from the early teenage years to the those in their late sixties, we each began our own separate paths to an exclusive period in our lives when we all qualified as having severe disorders. One of us was in college, one in our early adulthood, and one a senior when we reached the severe disease threshold on the continuum of the disease.

The point is we did initially and clearly make a personal choice to drink experimentally as a large majority of our population does. In our minds, like most, the experimental became the recreational, the social experience.

We were attracted to the pleasure, the positive reinforcement we received from drinking. None of us had any initial awareness or conscious realization of our genetic predisposition, and therefore a higher brain sensitivity to alcohol. The binge drinking at first, we thought, was just a bit of overusing social use.

Then, at some point in our drinking experiences, we each became, on our own timeframe, unable to consciously decide to drink less. We suspected, but fearfully did not want to admit, we could not stop drinking for any sustained length of time. We realized we were experiencing problems.

We each tried to control our intake, but we each arrived at a "capture" point where the desire for stress or pain relief was now manifesting itself as a negative reinforcement. The wanting, the *need* for alcohol, both its seeking and its consuming, overwhelmed us.

THE TREADMILL, THE SILENT ASSASSINS, AND THE SLEDGEHAMMER

I describe the mental imprisonment of the addictive cycle by saying I was on a treadmill that was spinning at a speed too fast to keep up with, but too fast to jump off. I was being torn apart with one foot on the speeding treadmill and the opposite knee scraping on the ground! Stuck on the treadmill of addiction and its cyclical stages of tolerance, withdrawal and cravings, is progressive torture. A lonely imprisonment of the soul!

The legal drugs of alcohol, nicotine, marijuana, prescription painkillers, and other over-the-counter substances are "the silent assassins" in our society that usually build up physiological dysfunction and adverse consequences. The damage done by these legal substances occurs over time, so often unnoticeable to the drinker or user in the beginning phase of use.

As a sledgehammer drug, legal substances like alcohol pound you over and over for a considerable period of time. The silent assassins often do not initially reveal the considerable brain and other internal organ damages that are developing without warning. US culture encourages using these easily accessible, socially acceptable, slower moving, silent sledgehammer assassins.

If a substance doesn't kill you fairly quickly, it can't be that dangerous! Wrong! Check out how many accidents, acts of violence, suicides, organ disease damage, other premature deaths, and damaging costs and consequences are silently, steadily, devastatingly attributable to repetitive legal drug intake.

Ironically, one of the nearly 40 percent of socially acceptable, legal substance consumers in our nation are, at some point, problem drinkers and users. When an individual begins to suffer disease symptoms and causes a degree of emotional or physical harm, the acceptance of the legal drinking or drug use by that individual, initially publicly encouraged, is now chastised as behavior beyond acceptable social standards.

How many of us as legal substance consumers unintentionally commit harmful behavioral, physical, medical damage and/or criminal acts, even fatal mistakes, while being high or in the throes of withdrawal pain? "Feeding the beast" is an expected, even encouraged social behavior until "the beast" demands more than what approximately 40 percent of American adult drinkers can afford to consume without experiencing or causing at least some level of harmful consequences to themselves or others.

The point is that we can readily see and feel the tragedy of a young person suddenly dying of a fentanyl-laced overdose. However, the chronic damage or even the acute consequences of our legal mind-altering substances are often undetected, disguised, silently devastating, a much more punishing syndrome of disease over time.

How many annual accidents, illnesses, and deaths do you suppose are actually related to the silent assassins beyond those officially reported or attributed to legal substance use? I know, just in my own drinking history, I dangerously drove a vehicle under the influence hundreds of times, which was unquestionably irresponsible, threatening my life and many others, without being arrested or reported. Now we have drivers whose reactions are considerably and dangerously slowed by legal cannabis products as well. Hopefully, self-driving vehicles can't come soon enough. What's your guess of the percent of drivers on your roads now who are operating without full consciousness or an acceptable reaction capacity?

Most excessive drinking behaviors, and there are many, are not occurring or discernible to the public eye, but are quite often intrusive or aggressive actions that are harming others or ourselves. We hear about an unexpected fatal accident or a crime of abuse, or we read of a 55-year-old person who dies prematurely from an illness or disease.

However, we don't always consciously connect these quiet privately occurring but harmful behaviors directly to the effects of our legal substances. Hypocritically, these drugs are socially acceptable, as long as their use consequences are unnoticeable. As long as we "drink responsibly" or "use safely and slowly," we are socially acceptable. When we go past the intoxicating limit (which nearly 40 percent of adult drinkers do), it is also invisibly, but methodically, adding to the slow creep of damage to our brain and body organs.

If you are a person who can have a drink and chill, fine. But the hard data indicates you are in the minority. You don't have to be a daily drinker to qualify as out of control. Just attend a pro, now even college, football game stadium. Money talks, drinkers drive!

"USING RESPONSIBLY" NOT THE NORM

Drinking, smoking, vaping, or using any prescribed mind-altering substance without hurting ourselves or anyone else in some manner, or without acting inappropriately, is not the norm! It is the exception statistically. Whatever mind alteration you choose is almost uniformly attached to the increased potential of creating some sort of physical or psychological harm. If you do the math, using the data of basic US adult drinking habits, only around 27 percent of those who use alcohol at all do not experience or cause reported (such as suicides, divorces, crimes, etc.) negative consequences.

There are many more incidents of anger, abusive behavior, personal and domestic conflicts, crimes, and violence resulting from alcohol or other legal drug use than those that become evident or are reported. This underreporting is especially the case when professionals administer surveys or a clinical screening of alcohol or drug use. How many people answer accurately and honestly about the extent of their substance use? Who of us are both conscious of or truthful about—or are even aware of—the extent of damage caused by our own drinking, smoking, or even prescription use?

A PATH TO DYSFUNCTION

A brain disease like alcohol use disorder or other substance use disorder is activated subsequently by normal experimental, recreational, and social use and develops with accelerated problematic use. With continued or extended drinking or drug use, the disorder begins to become entrenched in the brain and other body systems. This gradual dysfunction occurs with periodic or regular binge drinking habits, just as it does with the more noticeable daily "maintenance" use.

Eventually, conscious choice disengages in the dysfunctional "thinking" region (prefrontal cortex) of the brain. Rational deliberation is no longer possible, yielding to "default" decisions about whether to drink or use drugs now being made in the evolutionary primitive fight-or flight region of the brainstem. Subconscious acts to chase another drink or drug, rather than depending upon a conscious or rational decision, become the dysfunctional norm.

The more rational prefrontal cortex in the brain is, in essence, eventually switched off by chemical and structural dysfunction. The disease or substance disorder overwhelms a sense of rationality or reality with a chronic, cue-induced, "programmed" impulse.

The "modern disease model of addiction" accurately describes how certain people, with continued or extended use, predictably move along a progressive spectrum from experimental, recreational, and social drinking or use to substance misuse, and then to a moderate to severe substance use disorder. The level of the disorder is based upon specific medical criteria established by the American Society of Addiction Medicine (ASAM), the American Psychiatrists Association (APA), and the *Diagnostic and Statistical Manual of Mental Disorders* (DSM-5). The term "substance misuse" is used interchangeably with an initial "mild" disorder diagnosis. The term "addiction" is used interchangeably with "substance use disorder" and its three cyclical stages: tolerance. withdrawal and craving.

Once a person enters the habitual cycle of a substance use disorder, they will predictably experience three interwoven physiological stages (regardless of the mind-altering substance/s used). Their brain and body will

- undergo an increase in tolerance for alcohol or other drugs,
- experience acute or protracted withdrawal symptoms after brief or lengthier use stoppage or interruption, and
- eventually develop compulsive urges or craving for seeking a drink or other drug.

The stages of physiological occurrences with SUD are physical, predictable, and essential determinants for the primary diagnosis and treatment of the disease. The stages are intermingled, not always occurring in the same order. If you don't understand how these physical stages operate, it is difficult to thoroughly learn what addiction represents to the brain and body in effect, adaptation, and functional or structural changes over time. And each person is different physiologically and psychologically in how they respond to mind-altering and body-threatening chemicals. Each has their own level of sensitivity.

THE KNOWN CAUSES AND STAGES OF SUBSTANCE USE DISEASES

Substance addiction affects the physical, psychological, social, mental, and spiritual nature of each person differently. Quality treatment varies based upon individually assessed needs. And yes, culture, environment, age of onset, substance availability, and other causal factors come into play.

There are a lot of basic similarities in patients addicted to any mind-altering substance, starting with a similar physiological pattern that most people on the spectrum of addiction disorders experience to some degree.

Modern science has identified a set of causes for substance addictions. And although each person has different degrees of external and internal influences related to addiction in their individual brains and bodies, enough scientific consensus has identified the primary causes of the disease and its physiological characteristics. The drug used, individual physiology, genetics and epigenetics, and cultural and environmental factors play significant roles in disease development.

The stages of the disease, the effects of particular drugs, and the brain adaptations to the specific drug used are all now more predictable, thanks to recent neurological research. This means there is not a "one size fits all" treatment but that the basic knowledge and effective standards of treatment protocols are now available to promote a comprehensive recovery. The desired outcome is placing the diseases of alcohol use and drug use disorders into remission. We now have the neurological and treatment knowledge to achieve this objective. We are excited to share this information!

This handbook does not offer you a "cure" for SUD. Today there is no known cure. Nor is there a way we know of to help you "control" your drinking because it goes against the basic physiological principles of the brain itself, as well as the practical experiences of every alcoholic or addict we have met.

The modern disease model of addiction, which is supported by the vast majority of the research and medical community, is the beginning of an elemental, yet critical grasp to learn how to work holistically to reduce the suffering of such a misunderstood disorder. It's the best place available to start real evidence-based progress of learning about the progressive nature of substance use disorders.

Contrary to the assumptions and myths still alive that promote a pervasive and harmful cultural stigma, it is unquestionable that brain chemistry and brain function change considerably with even moderate or minimal alcohol use. The greater the use, the more likelihood of brain damage.

Instead of the "weak willpower" cause of addiction suggested by the old fashioned "moral model of addiction," in the disease model, various normal thought-and-reaction processes of the brain are physically "hijacked." Cognitive thinking and responsible life responses to events become difficult. At some point in the development of substance addiction, the drinker or user is not consciously making the decision to drink or use. That decision is being made for them by the disease's dysfunction. The drinker or drug user and their brain are maladaptive. That is, they become "less than," disconnected, captured by their brain's chemical and structural dysfunction.

Fortunately, over time, the adult brain can also significantly recover from much of the damage done to it by alcohol or drug addiction. Through abstinence, the "rewiring" of brain cells and neural pathways creates "new learning" that leads to healthy behavioral responses that were absent during active alcohol or drug use.

Definitions Of Addiction

> **COACHING TIP**
>
> Definitions of addiction vary depending upon the professional perspective of the definer. Here are several varying descriptions. It is important to obtain a comprehensive overview of viewpoints on addiction to understand its multifaceted reach. The word *addiction* comes from the Latin word *addicere*, which means "to bind or give a person to one thing or another." Here are various perspectives.

A medical viewpoint:

> "Addiction is a treatable, chronic medical disease involving complex interactions among brain circuits, genetics, environment, and an individual's life experience. People with addiction use substances or engage in behaviors that become compulsive and continue despite harmful consequences."
>
> —The American Society of Medicine

A Merriam-Webster dictionary definition:

> "Addiction is a compulsive, chronic physiological or psychological need for a habit-forming substance or behavior having harmful effects."

A psychiatric viewpoint:

> "Addiction is a complex condition, a brain disease that is manifested by compulsive behaviors or substance use despite harmful consequences."
>
> —The American Psychiatric Association

An addiction physician/bioethicist viewpoint:

> "not a thing that happens to you, but a deeply personal phenomenon involving a strong, compelling desire…profoundly ordinary, a way of being with the pleasures and pains of life…a central human task to face suffering, addiction is a part of us"
>
> —Carl Erik Fisher, <u>The Urge: Our History of Addiction</u>, 2022

SCOUTING THE OPPONENT: ALCOHOL AND OTHER SUBSTANCE USE DISORDERS

A public definition:

> "Addiction is a brain disorder characterized by compulsive engagement in rewarding stimuli despite adverse consequences."
>
> —Wikipedia

An educational viewpoint:

> "In a sense, addiction is a pathological form of learning."
>
> —Antonella Bonci, <u>The Science of Addiction: The Addicted Brain</u>

A Buddhist viewpoint:

> "The root cause of all addiction is the illusion that life is controllable and the delusion that we are in control. Addiction is attachment which brings suffering."

An addiction medical practitioner/author viewpoint:

> "It's not the activity or object that defines an addiction, but our relationship to whatever is the external focus of our attention or behavior . . . in which a person feels compelled to persist regardless of its negative impact . . . The distinguishing factors of any addiction are compulsion, persistence, preoccupation, relapse, impaired control, and craving"
>
> —Maté

Another physician viewpoint comes from Dr. Maté, who also references a "common addiction process":

> "The addiction process governs all addictions and involves the same neurological and physiological malfunctions. The differences are only a matter of degree. All addictions share states of mind such as craving, shame and behaviors such as deception, manipulation and relapse. On a neurological level all addictions engage the brain's attach-reward system and incentive motivation system which escape from regulation by 'thinking' and impulse-control areas of the cortex."
>
> —<u>The Realm of Hungry Ghosts</u>

A spiritual viewpoint:

> "All human beings have an inborn desire for God; whether we may experience it as longing for wholeness, completion, or fulfillment, it is a longing for love, a hunger to love, be loved, and move closer to the source of love. This yearning is the essence of the human spirit."

> "The longing at the center of our hearts (for love) repeatedly disappears from our awareness…and is usurped by forces not at all loving. Our desires are captured…addiction attaches desire, bonds and enslaves the energy of desire to certain behaviors, things, or people. These objects…become preoccupations and obsessions to rule our lives."

> "Attachment fuels our desire to specific objects and creates addiction…the most psychic enemy of humanity's desire for God (and love). Addiction makes idolaters of us all, by forcing us to worship objects of attachment. Addiction is attachment to anything other than our creator and love."

> —Gerald May MD, <u>Addiction and Grace</u>, 1998

An addiction medical specialist viewpoint:

> "A primary, chronic, neurobiological disease with genetic and environmental factors influencing both its development and its manifestations. It is characterized by behaviors including one or more of the following: lack of control over drug use, compulsive use, and continued use despite harm and craving."

> —Dr. Richard Whitney, Medical Director Ohio Professional Health Program (OPHP)

Definitions of Substance Addiction (Substance Use Disorder)

Definition of Substance Addiction or SUD

> "Regardless of the mind-altering drug recurrently used, substance use disorder (SUD or substance addiction) is a primary, multifaceted, and often treatable disease of the brain and body that is chronic, progressive, relapsing, incurable, and fatal, if untreated. SUD is predictable, characterized by a recurring interwoven cycle of tolerance, withdrawal symptoms with a

negative emotional state, and a craving or compulsion to drink or use drugs despite harm, loss of control, other cognitive dysfunction, pathological organ damage, and loss of life connections and relationships."

—Coach Greg Wince

Substance use disorder interrupts reality and often disables physical, mental, psychosocial, and spiritual development. Consequently it can be appropriately labeled as a "learning, memory, motivational, thinking, social, and emotional disease" because all regions of the central nervous system, including the brain neural pathways, chemicals, receptors, and functions, and most body organs, are adversely altered or diseased by significant drinking or drug use.

Other Definitions of Substance Addiction

"A disease that affects a person's brain and behavior leading to an inability to control the use of the drug no matter how much harm it causes"

—Mayo Clinic

"Substance Use Disorders (SUDs) involve changes to the circuits of the brain that affect decision-making, impulses and the stress and reward systems. A chronic medical disease viewed for too long as a disease of choice and not a disease of the brain, but there's a clear biological basis for addiction. We place SUDs firmly in the category of medical and public health challenges, rather than a character flaw."

—"Facing Addiction in America" US Surgeon General Report of Vivek Murthy, 2017, Preventing Addiction

"Drug addiction is a chronically relapsing disorder characterized by:
- a compulsion to seek and take drugs
- a loss of control in limiting intake
- emergence of a negative emotional state where access to the drug is prevented (e.g., dysphoria, anxiety, irritability, anger)"

—Koob, Arends, and Le Moal Drugs, Addiction, and the Brain

"Addiction is a treatable medical disease involving complex interaction among brain circuits, genetics, the environment, and an individual's life experiences. People with addiction use substances or engage in behaviors that become compulsive and continue despite negative consequences."

—The American Society of Addiction Medicine (ASAM)

"Addiction is a complex disease of the brain and body that involves compulsive use of one or more substances despite serious health and social consequences. Addiction disrupts the regions of the brain responsible for reward, motivation, learning, judgment, and memory."

—Shepherd Hill, Licking Memorial Behavioral Health System

"A primary chronic disease of brain reward, motivation, memory, and related circuitry that leads to characteristic biological, psychological, social, and spiritual manifestations."

—The American Society of Addiction Medicine (ASAM)

"A chronic but treatable medical condition caused by changes to the brain circuits responsible for pleasure, reward, self-control, and feelings of stress."

—Dorri Olds, Addiction and Recovery, The Biology of Addiction

THE OPPONENT: FUNDAMENTALS

The History of the Public Perception Models of Alcoholism (now known as Alcohol Use Disorder)

The following is a brief history of the public perception of Alcoholism as provided by Shepherd Hill.

- **Impaired Model**–"Alcoholics can't Change"
  - Town drunk–food and shelter are often provided but no treatment is available. This springs from observation of late-stage alcoholism.
- **Dry Moral Model**: Introducing "Demon Rum"
  - Alcohol is evil. Good people don't drink. Springs from 19th century religions. There is no treatment because there is no illness. The alcoholic often experiences remorse and guilt. He needs to recognize his sinfulness, ask for help, accept his punishment, and once forgiven, rejoin the moral community.
- **Wet Moral Model**: "Social drinking becomes the goal"
  - Supports controlled drinking. Good people can control their drinking, bad people cannot. Becomes a matter of willpower; no concept of illness; the goal is to teach the alcoholic to drink within society's norms.
- **Psychoanalytic Model** – "Enter the Addiction Personality"
  - Assumption is that alcoholism represents a hidden psychological disorder. Personality structure

is responsible for a person's dependence on alcohol; therefore, treatment is directed toward the entire family rather than the individual.
- **Family Interaction Model**: "Family Treatment"
  - One family member is "selected" or "volunteered" to play the role of the alcoholic in order to meet the family's psychodynamic needs; therefore, treatment is directed toward the entire family rather than the individual.
- **Old Medical Model**: "Becomes a Real Disease"
  - Springs from dramatic increase of knowledge. The alcoholic has a genetic predisposition for this disease. The goals of treatment are education about the disease so that one can self-diagnose and then take responsibility for his/her self-treatment.
- **Alcoholics Anonymous**: Living Without Alcohol
  - Recommends abstinence. Alcoholics are "allergic" to alcohol. Self-help groups; it works for those who follow their suggestions; needs no justification other than it works

Diagnostic Criteria for Substance Use Disorder (SUD)

In the defining medical publication (DSM-5), the new diagnostic criteria emphasize compulsive use as the result of craving, as well as tolerance and withdrawal factors. Drug dependence and abuse are now combined medically into one continuum of substance use disorder (SUD), on a range of severity from "mild" to "moderate" to "severe" based upon the criteria listed below. Is the patient.:

- Taking the substance in larger amounts or for a longer period than intended?
- Wanting to cut down or stop using the substance but unable to do so?
- Spending a lot of time obtaining, using, and or recovering from use?
- Having cravings and urges to use the substance?
- Experiencing interruptions with work, home, school, or other relationship aspects of life?
- Continuing to use, despite consequences from use?
- Abandoning important social, work, or recreational activities because of substance use?
- Continuing to drink or use, even when they realize they have a problem?
- Exhibiting tolerance, which is needing more of the desired substance to obtain the effect they want?
- Experiencing withdrawal symptoms when they aren't drinking or when they are cutting down, and these symptoms can be relieved by more use of the substance?

A *yes* to 2 to 3 is considered "mild substance use disorder."

A *yes* to 4 to 5 criteria is labeled as "moderate SUD."

A *yes* to 6 or more criteria is "severe SUD."

COACHING TIP

Even as a supposed "high-functioning alcoholic," I was able to check all ten criteria from my experience drinking. Although my last drink was when I was fifty-four years old, I honestly could have checked all ten boxes on the SUD criteria at least twenty-five years before then!

Risk Factors Contributing to Substance Use Disorder

The following primary risk factor list can be used to determine whether a person has a likelihood of beginning substance use, including regular or harmful use; a substance use disorder; or other behavioral health issues. I can check off all seven in my history:

- Genetics/Hereditary/Environmental Factors
  - Family history (genetics and epigenetics) is a major factor in passing on alcoholic and drug addiction risk tendencies.
    Note: I recommend the following sources of information to help understand epigenetics.
    - genone.gov
    - The Developing Genome: An Introduction to Behavioral Epigenetics, D. S. Moore, Oxford University Press, 2015
    - NIH Roadmap Epigenomics Project, November 2019
    - "About Epigenetics", The Canadian Epigenetics, Environment and Health Research Consortium (CEEHRC)
  - How you lived through being in the womb, early infancy, child care, and other experiences as you developed in childhood and adolescence are all major determinants of risk.
- Age of initiation/onset
  - Because the brain is in its maturation stage until a person reaches their twenties, the earlier in life you begin to drink or use drugs, the more likely you are prone to addiction.
- Life experiences of trauma
  - Experiences of childhood abuse, witnessing of abuse, or living in trauma correlates to the higher risk of addiction. Trauma does not have to be physical or visible.
- Stress/anxiety
  - The more unmanaged stress or anxiety is in your life, the more likely you are to seek relief from pain. Stress is a leading factor in relapse after you have initially become abstinent from alcohol or drugs.
- Conditioning/learned behavior
  - Often, in certain environmental circumstances, we learn by our own experiences or the example of others to seek pleasure or pain relief through alcohol or drug use.

- American Culture promotes the use of alcohol or drugs to feel better, relax, and socialize. The government allows alcohol and tobacco, two of the most addictive and dangerous drugs to be legal and widely accessible. Availability of a mind-altering substance is a major risk factor for a substance disorder.

My Own Risk Factors for My Alcohol and Nicotine Use Disorders

Genetic predisposition (heredity), environmental factors such as childhood trauma, availability of the substance and the age of onset are primary factors in increasing the chances of developing a substance use disorder. In my case, I checked all five boxes.

Genetically, I had close relatives on both the paternal and maternal sides of my family that had significant alcohol and tobacco habits. My age of onset when I had my first drink and cigarette, was at age twelve.

In retrospect, I can also see how I experienced an unintentional environment of emotional trauma on several occasions in my younger life. I was loved by my parents and never was physically abused, but there were several unanticipated, major influences on my psyche that affected me as a child, and emotionally were carried into adulthood. According to addiction experts, unbeknownst to me, these traumatic periods significantly increased my odds of developing a substance use disorder.

According to recent science, surprisingly my initial trauma was in my prenatal and postnatal growth period when there is rapid brain development. Numerous studies show that maternal stress and anxiety during pregnancy can result in a range of problems for the offspring. Trauma for the mother can result in harmful, elevated stress hormone (cortisol) levels that reach the brain of the baby.

In pregnancy or in postnatal traumatic stress of the mother, the offspring is more likely to develop anxiety, ADHD, and subsequently, the increased likelihood of developing a substance use disorder.

The traumatic incident in my prenatal period was the separation anxiety of my mom. World War II was starting and my dad left for Europe months before she was fully aware of her pregnancy.

The postnatal trauma included her receiving the telegram of my Dad being shot in Germany several weeks before I was born. Obviously, this was enough stress to generate anxiety and devastating fear.

In my childhood at age nine and again at age thirteen, I also experienced months of alienation and trauma by being twice diagnosed with life-threatening illnesses. In these periods, both times I was hospitalized for weeks and then isolated at home for months.

You would think that the worst part of these two periods would be a fear of dying, and I'm sure that often impacted my emotional being for extended periods. However, the worst part of these traumatic experiences I remember was being separated from school and my friends, and being isolated and inactive for months on end, especially being prohibited from my greatest passion, playing sports.

The overwhelming sense of alienation led me to feel totally out of my element, out of control of my life and future. In a sense, I felt abandoned, and removed from life itself. Seeing other kids die during my hospital stays obviously made another mental imprint and the impression of being lost.

In hindsight, I can relate to feeling lost during my entire teenage years and into adulthood. I can now see how these "environmental" traumas impacted my emotional health and my opting to drink alcohol to ease that pain of separation. I am so grateful to my wife for sticking with me and for how she patiently and lovingly helped me through many emotional travails.

The Patterns of Drinking/Drug Use

Depending upon a multitude of risk sources, individuals develop different patterns of alcohol or drug use and may change from one pattern to another.

- Low Risk Drinking/Use: Consumption of an amount of alcohol or other drug below the amount deemed *harmful* and used in circumstances not considered *hazardous.* (Several recent studies indicate there is no such thing as no-risk use, and that even in small amounts, alcohol or some drugs can cause physiological damage to some people.) The term "moderate drinking" is no longer used in medical terminology.
- Non-Use: Simply not drinking or using mind-altering drugs at all (believe it or not, there are adults in the US who have never sipped, swigged, smoked, snorted, or shot up)
- Abstinence: A state of non-use often after a conscious decision to avoid all alcohol or drugs.
- Experimental Use: The initial testing of a substance to examine its taste, smell, and feel.
- Recreational/Social/Controlled Use: Drinking or using drugs in a limited, infrequent, and low-risk manner in the presence of others and with no harm caused.
- Unhealthy, At-Risk, Hazardous, Harmful, or Problem Use: Any use that increases the risk or likelihood or has already led to health consequences.
- Binge Drinking: Medically defined as a period of uninterrupted drinking of excessive amounts within a set time frame resulting in a blood-alcohol concentration of above 0.08, which is usually 4 to 5 or more drinks in a short period of time, on at least one day in a thirty-day period. Bingeing has many different connotations, including drinking 4 to 5 drinks once a week, twice a week, once per month, or twice per month.
- Heavy Drinking: Having five or more binge-drinking episodes in a month, or women having 8 or men 15 or more drinks on a weekly basis.
- Substance Use Disorder (Addiction): a pattern of drinking or drug use that involves the cyclical stages of tolerance change, a withdrawal syndrome, and compulsive cravings resulting in a loss of control, continued use despite harmful consequences, and a loss of connections. For a variety of definitions of addiction, see the previous section, Definitions of Addiction.

Modes of Heavy Drinking

- Maintenance Drinking: Drinking at a rate intended to obtain or maintain a certain level of intoxication, often done by daily drinkers who intend to escape negative withdrawal feelings.
- The "High Functioning" Alcoholic (Working Alcoholic): A person who is able to conceal and manage their addiction to stave off personal, professional, and legal consequences, at least temporarily. Here are signs of a "high functioning" alcoholic:
  - Denial of a problem
  - Drinking alone
  - Binge drinking
  - Drinking every evening
  - Maintenance drinking including morning or day drinking
  - Craving social gatherings/parties/traveling that typically involve drinking
  - Avoiding local public drinking
  - Joking about alcohol
  - Using alcohol to cope
  - High tolerance

> **🏀 COACHING TIP 🏀**
>
> I was labeled a "high functioning alcoholic…until I wasn't! In the end, I quit functioning almost entirely, except for functioning in the task of seeking booze daily.

The Normal Progression of Drinking Alcohol for Individuals Who Develop a Disorder

Individuals who develop an Alcohol Use Disorder typically start with experimental drinking and then progress in a predictable pattern.

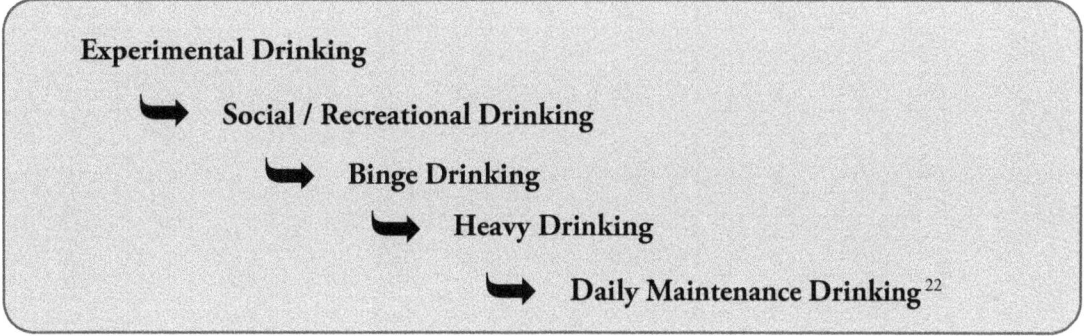

Experimental Drinking
↪ **Social / Recreational Drinking**
  ↪ **Binge Drinking**
    ↪ **Heavy Drinking**
      ↪ **Daily Maintenance Drinking**[22]

THE OPPONENT: STRATEGIES AND PROCESSES

The Most Common Signs and Symptoms of Alcoholism

The list below shows the most common effects of alcohol at varying consumption levels.

	External Signs	Internal Symptoms
At Low Doses	<ul><li>Personality Changes</li><li>Increased talkativeness</li><li>Expansive personality</li><li>Increased confidence</li><li>Improved mood</li><li>Increased assertiveness</li><li>Released inhibitions</li><li>Overreaction to real/ imagined criticism</li><li>Complaints of feeling poorly</li><li>Anorexia</li></ul>	<ul><li>Hangovers</li><li>Blurred vision</li><li>Loss of balance</li><li>Headaches</li><li>Sedation</li><li>Mild euphoria</li><li>Increased intolerance</li><li>Memory lapses</li><li>Withdrawal symptoms</li><li>Insomnia</li><li>Dysphoria</li><li>Beginning tremors</li></ul>
At Increased Doses	<ul><li>Pronounced mood swings</li><li>Emotional outbursts</li><li>Uninhibited, profoundly relaxed high-risk behavior</li><li>Distinct impairment in judgment</li><li>Motor dysfunction</li><li>Staggering</li><li>Slurred speech</li><li>Muscle incoordination</li><li>Slow reaction time</li><li>Decreased pain sensation</li><li>Bleeding</li><li>Vomiting</li></ul>	<ul><li>Sneaking drinks</li><li>Thinking impaired</li><li>Feeling guilty</li><li>Loss of interest, motivation</li><li>Blackouts with total memory loss</li><li>Severe tremors</li><li>Vomiting/fever/Diarrhea</li><li>Efforts to control drinking fail</li><li>Drinking alone</li><li>Dulled concentration and insight</li><li>Discriminatory ability lost</li><li>Learning and memory impairment</li><li>Mental confusion</li><li>Greater emotional instability</li><li>Severe withdrawal symptoms</li><li>Irritability/anxiety</li></ul>

SCOUTING THE OPPONENT: ALCOHOL AND OTHER SUBSTANCE USE DISORDERS

Late/Terminal Stage	• Agitation • Anesthetic level of intoxication • Stuporous but still conscious • Severely impaired motor function	• Decreased response to environment • Rapid dramatic mood change • Paranoia and phobias • Bleeding out of the mouth • Wernicke-Korsakoff syndrome
Fatal Stage	• Death	• Korsakoff psychosis • Delirium tremors (DTs) • Wet brain • Vivid hallucinations • Psychotic behavior • High fever

Predictable Outcomes of Untreated Substance Addiction

If a person with alcohol use disorder or drug addiction is untreated and does not go into remission from the disease, the following are highly likely outcomes they will experience:

- The loss of meaningful relationships (to jobs, marriages, other people, money, self and self-esteem, reality, spirituality, etc.)
- Arrest and incarceration
- Institutionalization
- Serious mental and physical health problems
- Premature death due to suicide, organ disease, accident, or violence

Note: The good news is that most people who suffer from alcohol use or drug use disorders are physically and mentally able to recover if properly treated before irreversible brain and organ damage is done.

Physical Damages of Alcohol Use Disorder (AUD)

The following are some physical damages drinking causes:

- Brain chemical and neurological pathway and structural damage to brain systems, including blackouts, foggy brain, brain poisoning, and brain size shrinkage
- Liver spots, fatty liver, liver disease, fibrosis, cirrhosis, and cancer
- Central nervous system impairment, stress system dysfunction
- Reproductive system impairment
- Muscular/motor dysfunction

- Heart and artery disease/heart function, irregular heartbeat
- Impacted blood pressure/heart rate cardiomyopathy
- Internal bleeding, pancreas and stomach damage
- Cancer of the head and neck, throat, esophagus, colorectal, breast, pancreas, liver, and brain
- Weakened immune system, increased stress sensitivity and anxiety
- Higher risk of depression, stroke, and sleep problems
- Loss of thinking, judgment, cognition, and decision-making ability
- Learning disability
- Disruptive emotional mood, motivational and behavioral changes

Examples of External Consequences from Damages

- Financial and legal problems
- Accidents/Injuries
- Crime/Incarceration
- Institutionalization
- Sexual assaults
- Drownings
- Loss of relationships – self, family, others, jobs, etc.
- Premature death
- Poor mental health
- High-risk behavior

Substance-Induced Mental Disorders

There are substance-induced mental health disorders—disorders in persons who did not demonstrate the problem before using alcohol or other substances. These include the following:

- Psychotic disorders: delusions, hallucinations, and paranoia
- Volatile mood swings from depression to mania, similar to bipolar disorder
- Depressive disorders: severe stress and mood changes
- Anxiety disorders: emotional/mental changes
- Sleep disorders: a severe change in sleeping patterns caused by the pharmacological effects of mood-altering substances
- Sexual dysfunctions: a disruption of the human libido (desire), excitement (arousal), and orgasm, functions of sexual response
- Delirium tremens: a condition caused by intoxication from a psychoactive substance, resulting in severe disturbance of focus and attention

- Neurocognitive disorders: a decline or worsening of normal mental abilities
- Persisting dementia: the lasting loss of mental ability caused by a gradual death of brain cells
- Persisting Amnesia: the significant loss of memory and interruption in the ability to form new memories or recall existing ones, often caused by alcohol or benzodiazepines

THE REASON I DRANK

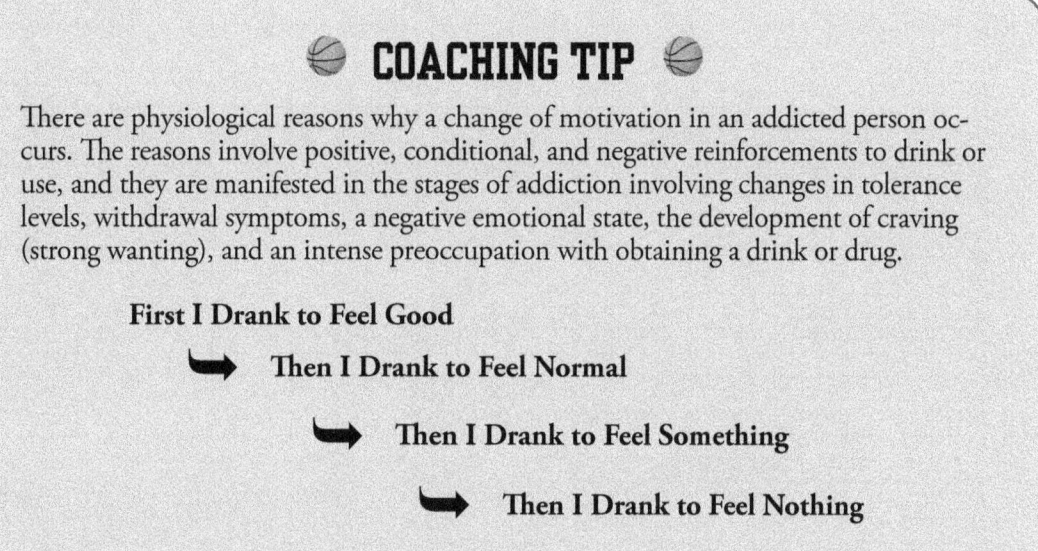

Alcoholics are not just career drunks or old-timers down on their luck, they are just as likely to be talented, intelligent human beings in the prime of their lives. We don't always know what hits us and why we continue to harm ourselves in spite of the pain resulting from our insistence of empty, fruitless, "pleasure-seeking." Our decision to continue this torturous process is the result of losing cognitive capacity and being driven by uncontrollable impulse.

THE PROCESS OF BECOMING ADDICTED TO ALCOHOL

- Alcohol is consumed, and initially the brain learns that good feelings result. A taste for what originally may seem bitter or even repugnant is acquired. A subconscious, positive association between alcohol and pleasure is established. This subconscious bond is strengthened with repetition, certain settings, routines, and rituals.
- Alcohol is quickly absorbed by the body and enters the brain where nerve cells, their neurotransmitters (such as GABA, glutamate, dopamine, serotonin, and noradrenaline) and the messenger/recep-

tor sites in the brain are altered in response to the drug. The brain is designed to maximize pleasure and minimize discomfort.
- Genetic factors, environmental factors, the age of onset of use, continued exposure to the drug, and many other individual factors influence the effect of the drug in the short- and long-term.
- The disease is activated with harmful use that involves a recurring cycle of tolerance change, withdrawals, and craving. Both brain disease and pathological organ damage may occur.
- Once the diseased brain reaches a certain "capture" point, the drinker cannot always consciously process a decision, but the drinker is habitually driven by the reinforcement of compulsive cravings and associative learning.
- The damaged brain now holds many physiological and psychological dysfunctions including mental confusion and distorted thinking, learning disability, memory impairment, motivational deficiency, and lapses in judgment. In addition to brain malfunctions, other pathological organ damages are occurring.
- The alcoholic or addicted person creates a distorted mental reality, including being in denial of their problem, while being unable to decide not to drink.
- Despite compounding negative consequences and critical losses of connection to life's relationships and reality, the alcoholic or addicted person continues to drink or use.

PHYSIOLOGICAL DIFFERENCES OF INDIVIDUALS WITH ALCOHOL USE DISORDER (AUD)

There are specific physiological differences that can preexist in the body and brain of an individual who develops AUD (compared to a drinker who does not develop an alcohol disorder) that make them more susceptible to the disease. The most obvious of biological differences are:

- Genetic pathways and epigenetic influences
- The level of cellular sensitivity to alcohol
- The ability of the liver to metabolize ethanol faster
- The phenomenon of "craving" with withdrawal

In addition to major cellular structural and chemical differences, according to Dr. Grisel, an alcoholic has about one and a half times the normal amount of beta endorphins in their blood, which relates to a sense of well-being. Also, Grisel references an innate opioid deficiency, differences in the concentration of ALPH enzymes found in the gut, considerable differences in brain chemistry like structural differences in the GABA receptor in the brain, and other suspected variations from human biological norms in the alcoholic brain.

Other significant differences that alcoholics possess may include:

- Less natural dopamine production

SCOUTING THE OPPONENT: ALCOHOL AND OTHER SUBSTANCE USE DISORDERS

- Lower levels of GABA (the primary inhibitory neurotransmitter) and glutamate (the excitatory neurotransmitter critical for learning and forming memory)
- Differences in gene expression and synaptic plasticity
- Stress sensitivity and variances in cortisol production levels
- Greater responsivity to alcohol-related cues characterized by autonomic response
- Variance in the amount of glucose, the energy provider in the brain
- Enzyme malfunction (may be why binge-drinking can lead to alcoholism)

Also a recent joint study at the University of Iowa (M. Potthoff, K. Flippo) and the University of Copenhagen (Gollum, Trammell) was published in *Cell Metabolism*, 2022. The study found that a hormone produced by the liver (FGF21) has genetic variants that are linked to increased alcohol consumption through actions in the nucleus accumbens (in the reward circuitry) and amygdala (the emotional center) regions of the human brain. This is another example of a potential physiological difference in some alcoholics.[23]

These and other possible physiological differences in the alcoholic's makeup are currently being studied and identified. The bottom line: people who develop an alcohol use disorder are likely made differently or develop certain biological variations from their environment. Because of these variances, along with certain psychological response mechanisms in the brain, certain people are more susceptible to a substance use disorder.

These and other possible physiological differences in the alcoholic's makeup are currently being studied and identified. The bottom line: people who develop an alcohol use disorder are likely made differently or develop certain biological variations from their environment. Because of these variances, along with certain psychological response mechanisms in the brain, certain people are more susceptible to a substance use disorder.

There are thousands of genetic variants that contribute to an individual's susceptibility for addiction. Dr. Danielle Dick, Director of the Rutgers University Addiction Research Center, delineates two "genetically influenced pathways" that impact how an individual human brain processes "risk, reward and emotion."[24]

The "externalizing pathway" describes how brains are wired for sensation and reward-seeking in individuals who engage in impulsive, risky behavior. These people are more likely to try addictive substances and develop problems.

The "internalizing pathway" describes how brains are wired to cope with fear and negative emotions. People genetically predisposed to internalizing are at greater risk for depression and anxiety. These specific genetic variants also predict a greater risk for substance use disorder. Dr. Dick indicates life experiences and environment can also mediate both of these genetically risky pathways.[25]

THE THREE CYCLICAL STAGES OF SUBSTANCE ADDICTION

Addiction evolves over time from impulsiveness, to compulsiveness, leading to a cycle of three stages: (1) the binge/intoxication stage, (2) the withdrawal/negative affect stage, and (3) the preoccupation/anticipation stage. The time it takes to become fully addicted, not just dependent on the substance, is also related to many factors, not the least of which is the type of drug taken. For example, the average period for heroin addiction is much faster than that of alcoholism. However, no matter which drug is involved, all substances of addiction follow the same three stages, which may be cyclical in nature.

The Binge-Intoxication Stage

The binge-intoxication stage largely is comprised of positive reinforcement through stimulation of the mesolimbic dopamine system in the brain. Increased tolerance develops with continued use. The amount of alcohol or drug usage increases in amount and frequency as the intoxication effect diminishes. This begins what we call "feeding the beast'." At this point, we become impulsive in our use, seeking opportunities to drink or use.

The Withdrawal/Negative Effect Stage

Another stage of substance addiction is known as the withdrawal/negative effect stage. Because of our brain adaptations to continued use of alcohol or drugs, when we aren't "feeding the beast," acute or protracted withdrawal processes can occur which create negative reinforcement to drink, as well as a negative emotional state, the one I call the "yuk" feeling. Developing brain damage and dysfunction add to the dilemma. Dependence upon the drug is firmly established and "feeding the beast" becomes involuntary.

The Preoccupation/Anticipation Stage

One other cyclical stage of substance use disorder is the preoccupation/anticipation stage, which is another name for extreme "wanting" or craving and planning the next drink or drug. This craving is both conscious and subconscious, involving the associated learning of feelings, triggers, and cues that stimulate even more the drive for the next drink. Dr. Kessler writes of the "capture point" in addiction where the natural human reward system is minimized, the thinking part of the brain is significantly damaged, and we are unable to decline the opportunity to drink or use, despite knowing it is harmful to us and others.[26] This is the stage that fully qualifies a person to be diagnosed with "substance addiction" on the severe end of the substance use disorder spectrum. At this stage, "the beast must be fed!" No choice!

TOLERANCE IN ADDICTION

> **COACHING TIP**
>
> Because of differences in how we digest ethanol (alcohol), as well as differences in our brain chemistry, other organ dissimilarities, and genetics, people like me develop tolerance to alcohol very quickly. Early on with our drinking, we become able to drink more and exhibit intoxication less—the so-called ability to "handle our liquor." Even tolerance has its limit over time.
>
> Toward the end of my drinking, I consumed nearly a fifth of gin or scotch a day and then, almost instantly, I lost almost all tolerance. Suddenly, at the end, I couldn't drink a couple of drinks without passing out.

Tolerance is a primary factor in the initial binge / intoxication stage. Generally, alcoholics are physiologically able to metabolize alcohol more quickly and efficiently, possibly because of differences in the liver and the adaptation capacity of the central nervous system. One of many potential brain and body differences in individuals who become addicted is in their ability to develop tolerance; ethanol metabolism in the digestive system is a physiological and genetic issue, not a learned or psychological response. The brains and bodies of alcoholics or addicts have structural, chemical, and molecular differences that can make them more susceptible to a substance use disorder.

Other Factors affecting Tolerance

- Tolerance is not caused by drinking or using too much, but rather it is the <u>cause</u> for increased consumption of a mind-altering substance.
- Tolerance on a cellular level is thought to occur due to the inactivation of certain cell receptors in the brain, making the substance less effective.
- Most alcoholics, upon significant consumption, notice an almost immediate ability to consume more than their peers and show less alcohol-induced impairment.
- Over time major changes occur in the neurotransmitter pathways of the brain, leading to impairment in judgment, memory disturbance, and emotional dysregulation.

WITHDRAWAL (ABSTINENCE SYNDROME) OF SUBSTANCE ADDICTION

> **COACHING TIP**
>
> Often painful physical and mental effects are experienced by a person after they stop drinking/using or significantly reduce their intake of a substance. Withdrawal symptoms can be acute in early abstinence or in a "protracted withdrawal," a prolonged abstinence period of weeks or months. Withdrawal is a diverse and dynamic process, considered to be "the trap" that keeps us in the addiction cycle. It is a punishing phenomenon and the primary factor in relapse.

Symptoms Of Alcohol And Sedative-Hypnotic Drug Withdrawal

The effects are numerous…

• Dilated pupils • Loss of appetite • Pale skin • Sweating • Clammy skin • Goosebumps • Diarrhea • Stomach cramps • Headaches • Stomach cramps • Shakes	• Tingles • Muscle and joint pain • Spasm • Mood swings • Agitation/hostility • Irritability • Anxiety • Depression • Panic • Increased heart rate • Vivid dreams • Nightmares	• Sleep disorders • Foggy thinking/memory loss • Physiological dependence • Psychological dependence • Pessimism • Urges/craving • Fatigue • Lack of initiative • Relationship problems • Stress sensitivity • Inability to focus	• Restlessness • Delirium Tremens (DTs) • Seizures • Extreme confusion • High or low blood pressure • Respiratory problems • Hallucinations • Fast Breathing • Fever

Acute alcohol withdrawal usually begins about 8 hours after your last drink and usually peaks 24 to 72 hours later.

Post-Acute Withdrawal Syndrome, a second phase of withdrawal symptoms, can occur within a few weeks to several months past the beginning of the abstinence.

CAPTURE AND CRAVING

> **COACHING TIP**
>
> How one responds to life's normal or stressful occurrences is very important. How we respond to life's events and conflicts determines who we are as a person. Do we think before acting? If so, under what conditions? Do we defer many of our decisions to "default" fight-or-flight responses? Do we choose short-term gratification and sacrifice our long-term health or reputation?
>
> By excessive drinking or drug use, we are training our brain to drink or use more. The dysfunctional brain has a diminished capability to think clearly, essentially yielding to a default reactive mode.

Whether or not we are aware, every action is preceded by a thought or series of thoughts. If we are conflicted about what action (response) to take, we often use defenses to justify our actions, The internal debate, the cognitive dissonance, ends when we give ourselves permission to act based upon the psychological "defense mechanisms" we have learned. We create our own alternative reality!

A trigger to drink (such as a hot day) combined with a convincing defense mechanism (such as justification and minimization like "I deserve a cold one") leads to overwhelming craving, anticipation, and use. Learning how to stop this delusional thought process before the craving becomes an action to drink or use again is vital. In other words, to recover, to manage cravings and avoid relapse, we must learn how we are presently responding to life, then how we can change that mindset and thinking process to minimize capture and craving and relapse. We will address such changes related to recovery in Volume II of this series.

Dr. David Kessler, in his best-seller, *Capture Point*, explains the process in which normal judgment flees and the loss of mental control occurs:

"When we are drawn to a particular stimulus, we act in response to a feeling or need aroused by it (a cue). Every time we respond (like a drink to soothe) we strengthen the neural circuitry that prompts us to repeat these actions. As we continue to react in the same ways to the same stimulus over time (thereby sensitizing the learning, memory, and motivational circuitry of our brains), we create emotional and behavioral patterns.

"Our thoughts, feelings, and actions begin to arise automatically. What started as pleasure becomes a need. This process of "neural sensitization" occurs and grows stronger…It becomes increasingly difficult to resist its power…as if we are being driven by something outside of our own control.

'Capture' (by a drug) is often the source of great pain and suffering."[27]

Withdrawal signs and symptoms vary depending on the drug or drugs used. Also, individual brain adaptations or responses to a drug can differ significantly. As Kessler puts it, "What captures me affects who I am and who I am affects what can capture me. Our minds can seize us, compelling us to act against our will and reason." This is one reason people become so puzzled, so baffled by addiction.

Caroline Knapp identifies "the central tenet of addiction as a firm, undeniable, unalterable, conviction of need, a feeling cured by some stimulus."[28] "Craving" is the dire feeling of need for alcohol or another substance, while "Capture" is the state in which the diseased brain no longer consciously chooses, but based upon conditioning, drinks or uses emanating from impulsive midbrain responses. The cortex, the more advanced thinking/reasoning region of the brain is minimized or bypassed. Like everything else in addiction, craving is progressive. In her book *Dopamine Nation*, Dr. Anna Lembke describes the critical relationship between pleasure and pain in the phenomenon of craving.[29]

Lembke indicates "that pleasure and pain are processed in the same area of the brain where pleasure and pain work like opposite sides of a balance." She relates "this moment of 'wanting' as the brain's pleasure balance tipped to the side of pain…the secret to finding balance combining the science of desire with the wisdom of recovery."[30]

The science Lembke refers to (she spells it out in chapter three of her book) highlights the major role dopamine and other neurotransmitters play in addiction. Her assertion is that dopamine "plays a bigger role in the motivation to get a drug reward than the pleasure of the reward itself." She maximizes the importance of the "seeking and anticipation" ritual of the next drink or hit.

Lembke states that "the more dopamine a drug releases in the brain's reward pathway and the faster it releases the dopamine, the more addictive the drug." She describes this urge for dopamine as "wanting more than liking."[31]

"Capture," according to Dr. David Kessler, is the result of "learning and memory associations to past experiences." The theory is that (1) a stimulus grabs our attention, (2) a lack of control is perceived, and (3) the brain/body undergoes a change in its emotional state. Based upon past experiences, "craving insures impulsivity, loss of inhibition, and compulsivity. Every time we respond to the stimulus, we strengthen the neural circuitry to repeat the same action."[32]

Addiction is, at a point in its development, not a choice! It is a disease that targets organs, with a cause and a known set of symptoms. Your brain manufactures chemicals that perpetuate a survival response and the midbrain sends out cravings for the alcohol or drugs. It deems them necessary for "survival," which is a primary evolutionary goal of all human beings.

Knapp asserts that in the later stages of alcoholism "the balance of pleasure and pain . . . tips precariously; pleasure becomes short-lived, pain is ever present. The only gratification (upon capture) is the redemption of just a few moments, from the physical, emotional, and spiritual agony that accompanies every waking moment. Getting alcohol to the cells is the only priority. The end result is widespread cell distress and panic. The brain cells are starving for alcohol!"[33]

With hyper-activated, agitated cells, the alcoholic drinks because it feels awful to stop. Capture and craving! Cravings for our drink or drug of choice can last weeks, months, or years, even in their abstinence. They can return after considerable time, but they can also be treated and diminished with help.

Shepherd Hill recommends following these "3 R's" to deal with cravings.

- **Recognize the craving early.** It is a lot easier to treat a low level 1, 2, 3, or 4 craving than a higher

level 6, 7 or 8. If you wait until you are overly obsessed with drinking or using to go to an AA meeting, it might not do much good. If you go because you find you are having intrusive thoughts at work, the meeting may well greatly reduce these.
- **Reduce the craving.** You do this with relaxation exercises, physical exercise, talking to someone or any activity which is designed to change the way you feel at the moment. You cannot reduce it by using. Each time you treat a craving by drinking, smoking a joint, etc. it comes back again soon, stronger than ever. One of the best methods for reducing cravings is a snack of cottage cheese or something that slowly releases sugar.
- **Re-Focus.** Cravings are a natural part of the recovery process. They do not mean you're going to relapse, or you are hopeless and should give up trying. Go back to what you were doing as soon as the craving passes, assuming what you were doing didn't cause the craving in the first place.

PHYSICAL CONSEQUENCES OF EXTENDED ALCOHOL USE

This is a summary of the effects of drinking on the body.

- **The Brain**
    - Dysfunction including the natural reward/pleasure system, memory, communication pathways, stress reduction, sensory system, and executive brain functions
    - Possible brain shrinkage or atrophy
    - Damage to neurological connections and pathways, altering both brain structure and function, possibly permanently
    - Cognitive and coordination dysfunction
    - Brain chemical imbalance related to stress, anxiety, and depression
- **Other Organs**
    - Damage to the digestive system, even bleeding; elevated liver enzymes; internal bleeding; fatty liver disease; and alcohol hepatitis and cirrhosis
    - Pancreatitis and pancreatic cancer
    - An enlarged spleen, which compromises the immune system
    - Heart disease, heart wall erosion, heart failure, high blood pressure, cardiomyopathy, arrhythmia, stroke
    - Widespread joint pain and deterioration
    - Damage to the long nerves and skeletal muscles, resulting in severe neuropathic pain and imbalance
    - Skin disease, including red splotchy face color
    - Increased likelihood of cancer including head and neck, throat, esophagus, colorectal, liver, breast, kidney, and pancreatic cancer

PHYSICAL CONSEQUENCES OF OTHER DRUG USE

- Accidental overdose
- Dirty needles leading to deadly infections such as hepatitis C and HIV, as well as skin and heart valve infections
- Damage to brain and neurological connections and pathways altering both brain structure and function, possibly permanently
- Increase in heart rate, blood pressure, breathing rate, and body temperature, as well as heart attacks (especially with stimulants)
- Kidney disease, lung problems, and liver disease
- A hole produced in the lining of the nose (intranasal from snorting cocaine)

SOCIAL AND EMOTIONAL CONSEQUENCES OF ALCOHOL/DRUG USE

- Loss of connection and realistic relationships with yourself, other people, the natural world, and any spirituality
- Family dysfunction, tension, separation/divorce, arguments, violence
- Depression, anxiety, mood swings, and increased isolation
- Increased irritability and anger
- Insomnia
- Performance loss at job, work, or school
- Psychosis, including paranoia
- Loss of interest in normal rewards, activities
- Legal consequences
- Family members developing coping mechanisms in their personalities to psychologically deal with the addicted person, or to "enable" the person to maintain certain patterns of drinking or drug use without certain consequences

SPIRITUAL CONSEQUENCES OF ADDICTION

- Loss of connection to normal life and important relationships
- Loss of connection to our own "self" and our integrity
- Loss of connection with joy, beauty, and other spiritual dimensions
- Lack of mental, emotional, and spiritual growth
- Uncomfortable feelings: boredom, regret, shame, anger, irritability, and despair
- Urges and uncontrollable cravings capturing our total being in an obsessive hunt for the next drink or drug

> **COACHING TIP**
>
> A loss of faith and hope in life occurs, even subconsciously knowing that our life is totally captured, focused on our compulsion to drink. The absence of our "true self" creates what we in recovery call "the hole in the soul," the spiritual vacuum. In his Confessions, Saint Augustine said, "to really know a person, don't ask them what they think or what they believe, find out what they love!" He was right on! I loved alcohol!

THE OPPONENT: THE FULL COURT PRESS

The Relapsing Nature of Substance Addiction

> **COACHING TIP**
>
> Why do we drink or misuse drugs when we know it is harmful to us and others? Why drink again when we just earnestly promised not to? Nevertheless almost every person with a substance use disorder will tell you they have repeated these scenarios countless times. It's because alcohol or other substance addiction is a chronic, progressive, relapsing disease, unless properly treated.

Relapse is a primary characteristic of the disease of addiction. With the aid of the conditioned learning process, relapse occurs for several primary reasons that include cue-induced reactivity and environmental triggers. Both prompt associated stimuli to reengage in a behavior or to think about related things. An increase in physiological arousal and the effects of withdrawal result in the development of cravings—urges to drink or use drugs. The result is that the brain's impulse system acquires greater control over behavior. The impairment of inhibitory control occurs, and consequently the brain is "captured."

Some call a brief relapse a "slip", which is an appropriate description. Alcoholics "slip or slide" back into their drinking. Unfortunately, the "slide" often becomes long-term. Relapses are mentally and physically conditioned by memory. Triggers and behavioral cues cause a return to the chase of a momentary reward, regardless of the anticipated pain created with relapse.

Alcohol disorder is often described as "cunning, baffling, and powerful" because the person who drinks again has no conscious intention to do so. He or she drinks because of their dysfunctional thinking and memory, physical or emotional triggers, behavioral cues, and a damaged stress-reactivity system.

With relapse comes a cadre of mental defense mechanisms learned by the alcoholic to justify more drinking. The cast of these defense mechanisms is numerous, spearheaded by denial and rationalization. The person drinking alcohol is in a defensive state might compare himself positively to a skid-row drunk, in order to rationalize and minimize his own predicament. Or she might tell herself she will limit her drinks this time. In any case, relapse leads to more drinks, more often.

As Dr. Lembke summarizes, "The pursuit of pleasure leads to the inability to enjoy pleasure of any kind. In addition, our normal rewards system is lost in our search for that fleeting sense of pleasure we once obtained from booze or drugs. Lembke indicates there is (at some point) . . . no high anymore. Yet if they don't get their drug, they feel miserable." She refers to "a pleasure-pain balance tilted to the side of pain …which drives people to relapse. We crave our drug just to feel normal."[34] Dr. Koob calls this phenomenon "dysphoria-driven relapse."[35] I call it "Yuk."

Physiological Causes of Relapse

In their masterpiece on addiction, *Drugs, Addiction, and the Brain*, Koob, Arends, and Le Moal describe the general conditioning constructs of relapse in the preoccupation/anticipation stage of the addiction cycle. A key fact is that more than 60 percent of people with addiction who stop using a drug begin using it again within a year. Relapse is the norm with this chronic disease.

Types of Relapse

Drug-induced reinforcement: The drug-seeking behavior following a prolonged drug-free period is associated with long-term behavioral sensitization. Behavioral sensitization plays a role in incentive motivation for seeking drugs.

Cue-induced reinforcement: Environmental cues paired with self-administration of alcohol or drugs can trigger a relapse. A cue could be anything associated with the behavior of drinking from "place conditioning," to "conditioned place preference," to seeing friends who drank with us, to viewing a TV ad, to ice clinking in a glass, and many more. This phenomenon is known as the "incubation of cravings" based upon conditions present with previous use.

Context-induced reinforcement: psychological mechanisms, occasion setters, excitatory and inhibitory conditioning that seek to modulate drug-seeking

Stress-induced reinforcement: Stressors elicit strong returns of drug-seeking behavior, and stress is the most likely trigger of relapse.

More on Relapse

Coach's Most Common Reasons for Relapse:

Reasons	Examples of Coach's Experience
Withdrawal	Binge drinking and feeling yuk, the many times I tried to stop or "drink responsibly"
Stress and uncomfortable emotions	Two full-time, publicly visible leadership positions; a growing family
Mental health issues	Depression (probably the result of drinking); anxiety attacks
People	Frat brothers, golf buddies, staff, coaches, business associates, etc. who I typically drank with
Places	A downtown restaurant-bar; my deck where I cooked out; conferences
Things or objects	Planes, ice clinking in a glass, music
Poor self-care/sleep habits	To sleep at 1:00 a.m., up at 6:15 a.m.; poor diet
Relationships/intimacy	Conflicts with wife, staff, parents
Pride/overconfidence	Winning (or losing); perfectionism
Boredom/isolation	Postseason separation anxiety being away from the team; the lack of daily grind off the "treadmill"

Triggers to Drink or Use Again

A trigger is a major cause of relapse, and stress is its energizing agent. Triggers can be external (environmental) or internal (thoughts, emotions).

Triggers are stimuli that prompt people to sense (most often subconsciously), think about, and/or engage in drinking or using. Certain environmental or emotional stimuli lead to a routine that becomes the basis of an ingrained habit.

Triggers are conscious or subconscious "reminders" to engage in certain behaviors. External or internal stimuli signal the midbrain (hub of the default "fight-or-flight" response) with memories that produce a state of stress and excitatory activation. The result is the brain seeks out old drugs, behaviors, friends, and locations that will relieve or diminish our stress.

The Trigger Process
- A certain stimulus triggers our memory
- A state of stress develops

- Our survival brain seeks old memories in search of a pure substance that will relieve our anxiety

Triggers include certain circumstances, times, locations, events, senses (sights, smells, sounds, feels, tastes), ideas or memories and certain emotional states.

The Shepherd Hill treatment team identifies five key triggers of substance addiction:
- Euphoric memory
- Environmental triggers
- Post-acute withdrawals (protracted, extended)
- Fluctuations in blood sugar
- Other drug use

CUES IN ADDICTION

Cues can be almost anything that leads to a routine that is seeking a reward. Habits of drinking create neurological cravings. Cues are a type of learned (conditioned) response and involve physiological (e.g., increased heart rate), and subjective reactions to alcohol or drug-related stimuli.

Early on, conditioning or habit-forming in substance use disorder is positive because the brain stimuli are accustomed to pleasure-seeking. Later in the development of the disease, with dysfunctional brain chemistry, negative conditioning (aversion) to find pain relief is established.

In *The Power of Habit*, a bestseller by Charles Duhigg, he explains that "cues are stimuli in the environment that lead to a routine as the basis of habit."[36] Incorporating this idea, James Clear identifies five primary cues that trigger a habit: time, location, proceeding event, emotional state, and people. The five human senses are integrated into these primary cues. Clear summarized "The Habit Loop" steps as (1) Cue to (2) Craving to (3) Response and to (4) Reward.[37]

A cue can be something visual, a certain time of day, a certain place, a sequence of thoughts, an emotion, event, or certain people. Duhigg says that "habits are powerful, but delicate…can emerge outside our consciousness, occur without our permission. They cause our brains to cling to them…so strong…at the exclusion of all else, including common sense."[38] "Liking" and "wanting" evolve into excessive cravings that force our brain into autopilot.

Cue Formation: A Three Step Habit Loop

Man is very much a creature of habit! The human brain is constantly looking for ways to save energy. An efficient brain "allows us to stop constantly thinking about basic behaviors. Our brain, in the basal ganglia, has devised a clever system to determine when to let habits take over. This takeover or so-called "capture" is the result of learning and memory. Only cues associated with past experience have any significance in triggering "cravings", the "I need it bad" feelings. Capture becomes an inevitable chain reaction in an addicted life.

SCOUTING THE OPPONENT: ALCOHOL AND OTHER SUBSTANCE USE DISORDERS

At the beginning of a habit like drinking, the brain spends a lot of effort looking for something that offers a hint regarding which pattern of behavior to use. This is a "three-step loop" process:

- *The Cue* - A trigger tells your brain to go into automatic mode and decide which habit is to be used
- *The Routine* - can be physical, mental, and/or emotional in nature
- *The Reward* - which helps your brain to figure out if this particular loop is worth remembering and using in the future

Craving is what makes cues and rewards work. Cravings power the habit loop. It is here that the brain begins to stop involving itself in decision-making. Over time the loop, repeated over and over, becomes more automatic. The cue and reward become intertwined in a powerful sense of anticipation and craving (stage three of the disease development). Choice disappears!

Examples of Dangerous Cues

> **COACHING TIP**
>
> My cues to drink were many and varied. Here are a few: The clinking of ice in a glass; TV/Movies with drinking (e.g., Leaving Las Vegas); a bar-restaurant sign; a phone call from a drinking buddy; an Ohio State football game; a golf course setting; certain music (e.g., "Rocket Man," "Scotch and Soda," "Deacon Blues"); an outdoor patio and grill; my wife's anger or any criticism of me in general; making a mistake in my job or coaching; a great win or any loss in coaching; out of town conferences; or plane flights; and many more.

Al J. Mooney MD., in his comprehensive *The Recovery Book* presents a terrific section on the behavioral cues that are dangerous to the substance-addicted person. They must be recognized and avoided or countered in recovery. Dr. Mooney refers to the terms for cues as "playgrounds, playmates, and playthings."

"Playgrounds" are specific places, often linked to our daily routines, that bring up old feelings and trigger cravings. "Playmates" are people you drank or used with. "Playthings" are the objects, images, or stimuli of the senses or emotions that bring on physical cravings.[39]

I was taught in recovery to identify and evaluate the "people, places, things, and events" in my life that I connected to drinking. Then I was told to spend my life elsewhere. The advice has served me well so far.

ADDICTIVE BEHAVIOR

> **COACHING TIP**
>
> Behavioral differences occur in alcoholics and addicts. These include behaviors caused by the substance, those caused by withdrawals, and those long-term personality changes from the extended effect of addiction on the brain.
>
> I remember a counselor telling me that once a person progresses along on the addiction spectrum they stop maturing and change into a different, unattractive, and unfamiliar person. With this deteriorating personality transformation comes a multitude of defense mechanisms, the greatest of which is "denial."

"The brain processes pleasure, the light, loopy, all is well, feeling of being buzzed. It's all just chemistry, this or that neurotransmitter . . . sending happiness along to neuronal circuits that never knew such joy before. There's a 'gravity of temptation' that overcomes 'the friction of your resistance.' The behavior becomes a habit, the habit a compulsion, and the compulsion becomes a life wrecking disease."[40]

The greatest obstacle to an addicted person is the inability to consciously admit a problem. Denying feelings, moods, and in essence, reality, the alcoholic develops a state of denial and a system of defense mechanisms that protects them and their drinking routine. By refusing to face disclosure, their greatest fear, alcoholics build a false self-image to defend themselves and their illusions. Dr. Harry Haroutnian has labeled this "malignant denial."[41]

> **COACHING TIP**
>
> On a deep internal level, alcoholics/addicts blame themselves and feel tremendous shame and guilt. Without understanding the disease, because they erroneously judge themselves of moral fault, they are reluctant to admit any problem and seek help. Then, of course, anyone admitting a problem creates a new threat to their ability to access drink or drug.
>
> We normally would prefer not to increase our personal accountability for the amount we drink or the problems we cause with our behavior by publicly announcing it. This is why it is vital that people trying to recover from addiction understand and recognize.

SCOUTING THE OPPONENT: ALCOHOL AND OTHER SUBSTANCE USE DISORDERS

The following are some of the key brain functions or areas that are adversely impacted by excessive alcohol/drug use that change behaviors:

- Voluntary motor control
- Learning related to procedures, habits
- The motivation and rewards system
- Natural rewards loss
- Memory
- Executive functions (time management, organization, task completion)
- Impairments in behaviors, inhibition, and compulsive behavior

The result of brain disorder is an increase in antisocial behavior including:

- Anger outbursts
- Manipulation
- Immaturity
- Irresponsibility
- Denial
- Dishonesty
- Silence/isolation
- Rationalization
- Deflection/blaming
- Procrastination
- Self-pity

Denial

> **COACHING TIP**
>
> In basketball, it's tough to score against a tenacious defense. When I was drinking I often thought this: "That was a mistake what I did last night. I drove the babysitter home, but I don't even remember doing it! That's not good! But I'm not going to mention it because my wife will hound me to quit drinking, and I really do not want to do that. If I had to quit, I would have no release from stress, no relaxation, nothing to do. To be honest, I love drinking and will let nothing take it away. Drinking is my best friend! What would I do without it?" In recovery, we refer to this scourge of denial as the river in Egypt, aka "da Nile!"

In his book *In the Realm of Hungry Ghosts*, Dr. Gabor Maté describes the **"Denial State"** of an addicted person: "Contrary to all reason and evidence, we refuse to acknowledge that we are hurting ourselves and others; we become completely resistant to asking ourself any questions at all." Maté describes what he calls "counter-will" to protect our resistance.[42]

A feeling of entitlement often led me to drink. I thought, "I work very hard and deserve a break, a chance to relax!" Many addicted high-achieving professionals, according to Dr. Haroutnian, "have delusions that they have few faults."[43] High achievers, like me, start to believe they are invincible and can effectively control their own environment. Professional arrogance (doctors and other leaders being particularly susceptible to egotistical illusion) feeds the need to be "a servant" of higher expectations and perfectionism. This self-delusion of high achievers leads to an extraordinarily, skillful development of self-denial and other defense mechanisms. Our delusion prevents facing the reality of our addiction.

Judith Grisel describes "cognitive dissonance as a big part of the denial engine." This term refers to the battle in the brain to create a response when cognition and behavior (our thoughts and our actions) don't agree. If we know taking a drink or two is not good for us, but imagine a drink would alleviate our stress, "the expeditious gratification is to change our cognitive thought and yield, default to short-term relief."[44]

Other Defense Mechanisms

 COACHING TIP

Alcoholics/addicts will avoid, at great cost, the reality of their own captured existence. We are blindfolded from our reality and use endless thought and behaviors to escape from facing the issues related to our disease that would, if exposed, cause us considerable angst. We prefer to deny and defend, rationalize, justify, blame, manipulate, and a host of other ways to delude ourselves.

Examples of defense mechanisms we manufacture to avoid reality include:

- Denial
- Rationalization
- People pleasing
- Projection
- Justification
- Fantasy
- Minimization
- Externalization
- Transference

SCOUTING THE OPPONENT: ALCOHOL AND OTHER SUBSTANCE USE DISORDERS

- Blaming
- Intellectualization
- Defocusing
- Sarcasm
- Undoing
- Regression
- Displacement
- Active negativism
- Passive negativism
- Changing the subject
- Manipulation

THE OPPONENT: THE DISCONNECTS OF THE ADDICTED PERSON

"Pain is in the Resistance"
-Buddhism

Loss Overwhelms the Addicted

> **COACHING TIP**
>
> Rev. Bruce Henderson, a dear friend and retired Presbyterian minister, once gave a memorable sermon on "The Ways We Get Lost." He articulated these ways of getting lost as:
>
> - Wandering about without any plan or destination
> - Getting poor direction, a faulty map or wrong path
> - Letting someone else lead us astray
> - Limiting our vision to hyperfocus on one way, our way
> - Getting captured or kidnapped
> - Becoming disconnected from reality

It is a combination of these ways of getting lost that a person with a substance use disorder becomes disconnected from reality. In *Lost Connections*, a *New York Times* bestseller, Johann Hari quotes Joanne Cacciatore from her research indicating that "pain is simply the result of a malfunctioning brain- makes us disconnected from ourselves, which leads to disconnecting from others. We are such a disconnected culture, we just don't get human suffering." I might add, especially we don't empathize with the pain of an active addicted person.

Hari's classic text lists nine basic causes of depression and anxiety. These causes are leading stress generators. The chances of stress becoming present in the life of an alcoholic or addict are multiplied exponentially as extended drinking or drug use continues. Hari's list of "disconnects" to real life, according to his research, are:

- Loss of meaningful work
- Loss of relationships with other people
- Loss of meaningful values or intrinsic motives
- Psychological issues from childhood trauma
- Loss of status and respect
- Loss of relationship with the natural world
- Loss of sensing a secure future
- The change in brain neuroplasticity
- Genetic switching (on and off) depending on what happens to you

To restore sanity and recover from the disease, an addicted person must restore these basic positive life connections.[45]

"Disconnect is the difference between the person you want to be and the person you perceive to be."[46]

NATURAL HUMAN GOALS VS. ADDICTED PERSON GOALS

There are vast differences between the naturally evolved goals of the human being and what becomes the primary goals of an active alcoholic or addict. Our natural human aims are:

- Survival
- Procreation
- Connection to ourselves, others, life itself and the divine

As a person becomes addicted their goals change to:

- possession (of the substance)
- power and control
- pleasure or pain relief

The human *needs* emanating from natural human *goals* are gradually ignored in addiction. Goals of the addicted person displace basic human needs with desire for the drug and any control they can exercise over their own life (which they intrinsically know is out of control). Displaced human needs during addiction include:

- Physiological needs: food, water, rest, warmth
- Safety needs: protection, security, order, law, stability, and freedom from fear
- Love and belonging needs: friendship, intimacy, trust, acceptance, affection, love, and affiliation

- Self-esteem needs: dignity, achievement, mastery, independence; the need to be accepted and valued by
- Aesthetic needs: the desire for beauty, pleasure, order, and balance
- Self-actualization needs: the realization of fulfillment of one's talent and potential
- Need for transcendence: the desire to move beyond ourselves and be motivated by helping others or driven by factors that do not personally impact them

Basic human needs become lost in deference to the drug-related goals of the addicted person

EFFECTS OF SUBSTANCE USE ON LEARNING, MEMORY, AND MOTIVATION

Key Brain Anatomy Related To Addiction

As a substance use disorder progresses, the neural pathways in most regions of the brain, the chemical balances in the brain, and the brain structures themselves are all damaged with continued use of alcohol or drugs. The thought center and the feeling centers of the brain are two key regions rendered ineffective or inefficient.

The prefrontal cortex, referred to as the brain's executive center, loses capacity. This region is responsible for most cognitive functions including decision making, planning, evaluating, judgment, problem-solving, organizing, and impulse control. Sexual and social behavior experience dysfunction as the cerebrum and other parts of the cortex shrivel up in an alcohol bath. Cognition pays a huge price.

The amygdala is a crucial neural circuit center instigating the emotions of fear, disgust, and arousal, and it prioritizes our conscious awareness. Our emotional brain circuitry links the amygdala with other neural networks that instigate learning, memory, habit, decision-making and motivation. These important functions also are rendered dysfunctional with extended substance use.

In addition, the brain's communication system is disrupted. As Urschel points out, "the brain is a communication, data interpretation, and storage device. Data is received from both outside and inside the body and sent through billions of neurons that must be able to 'talk' with each other."[47] This intercellular chemical messaging is accomplished by neurotransmitters, such as dopamine and serotonin. In order for this intricate communications network to function properly, the right kinds and amounts of neurotransmitters must be secreted at the right time in the right area with the right receptor cells. Mind-altering drugs interfere with all of these key systems of the brain.

Learning, Memory, and Motivation

The hijacking of the dopamine system by extensive alcohol or drug use isn't just associated with pleasure deficiency. Along with glutamate, it plays a major role in the impairment of learning, memory, and motivation. Initially, when alcohol or drugs provide the brain with large dopamine quantities, the brain learns to change many of its circuits associated with motivation and mood. Attention becomes exclusively focused on pleasure.

The ability to remember things from the past and learn new skills is dependent upon the quality of brain functioning. With substance addiction, memory gaps are characterized by short-term memory loss. Dr. Maté refers to "the automatic mind…which constantly interprets the present in light of past conditioning. With damaged cognitive function in the cortex region, new learning and new memory are replaced by a habit response."[48]

Additionally, the alcoholic or addict often has nutritional deficiencies which amplify mental confusion and memory loss.

>  **COACHING TIP**
>
> As alcoholics, we stop learning and growing emotionally. We drink our brains into a state of forgetfulness. Our motivation is subordinated to that one chemical urge for alcohol. The good news is that most damage to the brain can be mended in time with new learning and personal habit change.

Further Brain Damage

Continued use of alcohol causes a healthy brain to shrivel up. Much of the shrinkage is in the frontal lobe of the brain on the outer layer of the cortex, known as the "thinking" or executive center. The brain's communication system is severely disrupted, with damage to the neurotransmitter systems and their receptor sites.

With receptors "closed down," gamma-aminobutyric acid (GABA), a messenger that aids to keep you calm, is rendered ineffective. Considerable emotional and physical agitation occurs. Alcohol also increases glutamine receptor sites which can trigger seizures. Extended use progressively spreads physical damage throughout the central nervous system, and to other organs in the body.

The brain's sole energy provider, glucose, has its normal usage altered by alcohol. The limbic region of the brain which controls desires and the body's basic drives is altered by addiction. And the hippocampus, where most of the long-term memory cells are created, also experiences a marked decrease in overall activity and efficiency in an alcohol-damaged brain.

Many brain cells are destroyed, and all brain systems encounter some level of dysfunction. Recent research indicates that even small amounts of alcohol cause brain damage. Recent studies have also contradicted the popular idea that a drink or two daily assists heart health.

Alcohol's Specific Effects on the Brain

Here is what happens when alcohol reaches the brain:

- Alcohol turns on the GABA inhibitory system, so you can feel calm and relaxed.

SCOUTING THE OPPONENT: ALCOHOL AND OTHER SUBSTANCE USE DISORDERS

- The frontal cortex, the "executive" thinking region of the brain, is turned off by alcohol, impacting your judgment and behavioral control.
- Continue to drink more, and along with stimulating the inhibition of GABA, alcohol blocks the glutamate (energy) system that keeps you awake.
- Your blood alcohol concentration rises and affects many neuromodulators and neurotransmitters including serotonin (mood enhancer), dopamine (your drive, motivation, and energy), and endorphins (the body's pain-relieving system). Pleasure is related to the endorphins and dopamine interactions in the brain.
- Every brain region and functional system (thinking, reward, motivation, memory, energy, etc.) is affected by alcohol and the blood alcohol levels.
- Binge drinking initiates immune signaling and inflammation in the brain.
- When drinking continues, you lose memory, coordination, self-control, judgement, speech, reaction time, balance, sexual capacity, and more.
- Without stopping drinking at a 0.25 percent BAL, you experience confusion, disorientation, likely nausea and vomiting, and blackouts (loss of memory formation).
- With further drinking beyond a 0.5 percent BAL you can become unconscious, fall into a coma and stop breathing, death from "alcohol poisoning."

> **COACHING TIP**
> - Alcohol reaches equilibrium in the body and brain in less than an hour, but you can feel its effects just a few minutes after the first sip
> - Chronic exposure to alcohol undermines or lessens the self-medicating effects of the drug
> - The ability of the stomach and liver to metabolize the alcohol is based upon:
>   - The body characteristics and sex of the drinker
>   - The amount of alcohol and the amount of food in the stomach at intake
>   - The capacity of the individual to produce enzymes in the gastric fluid
> - The capacity of the liver and the health of other organs are involved in the system of alcohol metabolism

There are other drugs that produce effects similar to alcohol. These include sedatives, hypnotics, and tranquilizers such as "downers" and "sedaters" like barbiturates and benzodiazepines (e.g., Valium).

In each of these sedative-hypnotic drugs, the GABA inhibitory system is opened, which causes inhibition. These drugs all slow you down and an inhibitory neurotransmitter modulates every brain circuit and all behavior by slowing down brain activity, inducing muscular and psychotic relaxation, promoting sleep, and creating a sense of psychological distance from feelings.

STRESS AND ALCOHOL: THE DOUBLE WHAMMY

> **COACHING TIP**
>
> Stress is a primary "spiritual enemy" of an alcoholic or addict because it causes a vicious and destructive cycle. Stress causes the alcoholic to drink, and concurrently, alcohol excess causes more stress. It is important to understand how dangerous stress is to the addicted person, both as a cause and effect.

Alcoholics initially try to relieve stress by drinking. Learning more healthy ways to deal with stress is critical to our recovery. Stress can come at us from endless sources—people, places, things, events, health conditions, fatigue, lack of sleep, habits, feelings, thoughts, you name it.

Stress is, as Buddhists describe, the result of universal causes of suffering and is dependent on the way we respond to them. These stressful causes of suffering are: (a) the natural events of life (like birth, illness, loss, death), (b) the constantly changing nature of life, and (c) the realization of the impermanence of life.

A person in the throes of their substance use disorder has a "double whammy" of stress! This heavy dose of abnormal stress stems from both the lack of effective, efficient responses to normal life issues combined with the many self-initiated stresses the diseased behavior generates.

Addicted people become overwhelmed by stress and see no escape, except the temporary relief they get with the next drink or drug. In the recovery program, the dangers of stress are highlighted by the acronym HALT, which stands for Hungry, Angry, Lonely, Tired. These physical or emotional states are a signal that the alcoholic or addict is in the "stress danger zone" and needs to seek help.

The Biology of Stress

Stress is a physiological and psychological opponent, a primary trigger of addiction. In _The Addiction Spectrum_, authors Paul Thomas and Jennifer Margulis indicate that stress disrupts hormones produced by the pituitary gland in the brain as well as the common neurotransmitters like dopamine and serotonin. Hormones influence the production of these three essentials: (a) testosterone (which promotes energy and sex drive); (b) adrenocorticotropin (which stimulates the adrenal glands to make cortisol that aids in blood pressure, blood sugar, and stress management); and (c) a thyroid-stimulating hormone which aids in energy, brain development, and more. With chronic stress, this entire brain system starts to fall apart.[49]

According to author Harry Haroutunian in _Being Sober_, "Stress can be good or bad . . . all events of significance will stimulate the release of cortisol, which has the effect of raising the dopamine requirements in the person who has the addiction genes. Even positive experiences can be stressful."[50]

The overproduction of cortisol produces chemical changes in the brain that make substance addiction and mental illness more likely. According to authors Thomas F. Harrison and Hilary S. Connery in *The Complete Family Guide to Addiction*, "stress hormones can cause stem cells to be disrupted which, in turn, affect the way parts of the brain that govern rational thinking communicate with regions of the brain that govern learning and memory."[51]

Remember, some people are born with a greater genetic and biological susceptibility to the addiction process in the brain and also a greater sensitivity to stress. The combination of alcohol and stress is lethal! A fundamental slogan emphasized in recovery communities to help remind us of the danger of stress and to help us monitor our own reaction to it is "Easy does it!"

DRUGS AND THE BRAIN IN SUBSTANCE ADDICTION

> *"The fundamental role of the brain is to be a constant detector of the (external and internal) environment."*
> *- Judith Grisel* [52]

Recent neurological advances in brain imaging have had a tremendous influence on addiction studies that highlight these adaptations.

In Maté's *In The Realm of Hungry Ghosts*, addiction is said to represent a "different state of the brain", and drugs (including alcohol) temporarily change the brain's internal environment. Dr. Maté explains that addictive drugs resemble the brain's own natural chemicals "which allows them to occupy the brain cell receptor sites and interact with the messenger system operation within the brain and central nervous system."[53]

As Maté points out, "all commonly misused drugs temporarily enhance the brain's dopamine functioning."[54] The rates of dependency for each drug vary. Nicotine has the highest specific drug rate dependency, with one in three individuals becoming addicted. The next highest rate belongs to heroin, with nearly one in four getting addicted. Then comes cocaine, methamphetamines, alcohol, and marijuana, with those who try these drugs and eventually becoming addicted at a 12-20% rate.

Keep in mind that it usually takes a person, especially males, a longer period of extended drinking to become addicted to alcohol than other drugs take to reach a dependency stage.

Regardless of the substance, as Dr. Maté clearly points out, it simply requires three factors to converge for addiction to develop:

- A susceptible person
- A drug with an addictive potential
- Significant stress with preexistent vulnerability[55]

As you read on, you will find that, besides addiction having three cyclical stages, there are specific biological differences in people that lead to addiction vulnerability. Although the brain is diseased by addiction, in most cases it is eventually capable of being healed. The three basic laws of pharmacology show how drugs affect the brain, and the brain adapts to drugs by what is called an "Opponent Process Theory."

THE FUNDAMENTALS OF MIND-ALTERING DRUGS

"The opposite of addiction is not sobriety, but choice and freedom"
-Judith Grisel[56]

The Three Laws of Addictive Drugs

In <u>Never Enough</u>, Judith Grisel lists the three laws that apply to addictive drugs and stimulate the mesolimbic pathways of the brain. Those three psycho-pharmacological axioms are:

- The Law of Rate Change: all drugs act by either speeding up or slowing down neuroactivity; nothing new occurs in the brain because of alcohol or any other drug
- The Law of Side Effects: all mind-altering drugs have side effects and unlike normal brain chemicals, they are not targeted to specific brain circuits, but delivered from the blood throughout the entire brain and nervous system
- The Law of Brain Adaptation: the brain adapts to all drugs by "countering" them to achieve a homeostasis; if the drug speeds up the brain, an adaptation develops in the brain to slow down activity; and vice versa; the brain will adapt to speed up neural activity if the drug used is slowing activity

Grisel says, "the relationship between drugs and the brain is bi-directional". The drug impacts brain chemistry, and the brain's chemical response or adaptation to a drug is aimed at facilitating the opposite state.[57]

> 🏀 **COACHING TIP** 🏀
>
> Alcohol or other drugs impact the brain, and because the brain reacts to neutralize the impact of the drug used, brain dysfunction can occur as a result of repeated adaptation attempts.

SCOUTING THE OPPONENT: ALCOHOL AND OTHER SUBSTANCE USE DISORDERS

OPPONENT PROCESS THEORY

"The principal activity of the brain is making changes to itself." [58]

Principal

Pleasure and pain are processed in overlapping brain regions and work like a balance. Solomon and Corbett developed the Opponent Process Theory in 1974, introducing the idea that, just as the physical body utilizes the balancing process of homeostasis "adapting to conditions that alter its natural equilibrium," the homeostasis principle also applies to feelings and attempts to balance them.

Solomon suggested that all stimuli that disturb the way we feel are actively counteracted by the brain and nervous system to "refind" a psychological homeostasis. This applies to alcohol or drug intake, but it is not limited to these stimuli.[59]

The idea is that feeling states are maintained around a setpoint, just like body temperature, and any feeling, good or bad, represents disruption of stability or of a neutral state. Any stimulus (e.g., alcohol) that alters brain functions affecting the way we feel will receive a brain/body response exactly opposite to the stimulus. If the initial effect of a drug gets you excited, the brain will work to calm you down. If your drug slows you down, the brain will work to speed you up.

Dr. George Koob explains this adaptation to drugs as "the brain contains many feeling control mechanisms that serve as a kind of 'emotional immunization system.'" The system, according to Koob, "counteracts or opposes a change to an emotional equilibrium or neutral state, whether the variation to the normal or natural state is pleasant or disturbing."[60] The system of emotional balance helps to keep our mood in check even if the stimulus is strong. The brain is stronger when it's healthy. When it is repeatedly soaked in alcohol, it loses strength.

ALCOHOL HANGOVERS, BLACKOUTS, AND POISONING

- Hangovers
  - Primary Symptoms
    - Physical: fatigue, weakness, thirst, drowsiness, headache (due to dilation of blood vessels and dehydration), dry mouth, gastrointestinal issues, nausea, lack of appetite, vertigo, dizziness, clumsiness, balance problems, audio and photosensitivity (due to glutamate rebound), disorientation, shivering, sweating
    - Mental/Emotional: Concentration problems, apathy, agitation, anger, memory problems, confusion, guilt, regret, anxiety, impulsiveness
  - Methods of Treatment
    - There is no cure for a hangover, only methods of treating the symptoms, including: anti-inflammatory (ibuprofen with food), beta-blocker, hydration, food, caffeine, probiotics

- Blackouts
  - A blackout occurs when you drink so much (0.3 percent Blood Alcohol Content) you start to lose the ability to form memory. You are awake but have no or little memory of what occurred after you got drunk. This is not the same as "passing out."
- Alcohol Poisoning
  - This is the cause of people, especially young people, dying from excess alcohol. Alcohol turns on the GABA system of calming inhibition. Taken to its extreme, parts of the brain are totally inhibited (switched off) causing the loss of judgment or consciousness. With enough to drink, the brain is anesthetized and breathing stops.

> **COACHING TIP**
>
> We "learn" to acquire a taste for alcohol. We associate good feelings with the taste and smell of alcohol, as well as with the setting, routine, and/or ritual in which we drink it. In addition to this positive reinforcement of associative learning for alcohol, some people learn to like the "burn," the feel as the drink slides down the throat. Again this feeling is associated with the expected pleasure from alcohol. Many of us with an alcohol use disorder will tell you how much we loved both the thought of and the use of alcohol.

The Metabolism of Alcohol

The following are simplified steps alcohol goes through as it is broken down in the body and brain:

- Alcohol is absorbed through the walls of the stomach and the small intestine.
- Alcohol enters the bloodstream and goes to the liver where it starts to be broken down into acetaldehyde.
- A mixture of alcohol and acetaldehyde travel into the heart and the brain. Its effects are felt quickly in the body due to its fast absorption capacity.
- Alcohol allows the blood vessels of your skin to expand through vasodilation.

The Brain on Alcohol

There are around twenty billion neurons in the brain that serve as modes for messengers of our thoughts and processes, both conscious and subconscious. The chemicals that facilitate these messages and thus each of the brain's systems are neurotransmitters. The brain, it works like an "electromechanical machine" whose outputs include being awake, being asleep, storing memories, swallowing, thinking, and numerous other systematic functions.

Brain Fog

This is a condition in which the mind has difficulty with focus and understanding simple directions or questions. "Brain fog" can result in confusion and disorientation and is caused by excessive alcohol or drug use, withdrawal from drugs or alcohol, and underlying illness.

<blockquote>"More, Broader, Kinder, Earlier, Faster, Better, Longer!"</blockquote>

GAMETIME ADJUSTMENTS:
THE CURRENT STATE OF SUBSTANCE USE DISORDER TREATMENT AND RECOVERY

SUBSTANCE ADDICTION IS A PRIMARY, CHRONIC, PROGRESSIVE DISEASE

It is important to grasp the idea that addiction is a primary (physiological), chronic, progressive, and (if untreated) prematurely fatal disease. Our intent in this section is to:

- **Dispel old ideas and myths**, such as you can "think or behave your way out" of addiction, or handle the problem with your own willpower,
- **Prevent misdiagnosis or over-complication** of the diagnosis and treatment of a substance use disorder,
- **Eliminate unnecessary**, inadequate or excessively expensive **treatments**,
- **Reduce** numerous subsequent or repetitive **relapse** treatments, and
- **Sidestep misleading promises** of cures, "controlled drinking," or other attractive frills like exotic beach locations, riding stables, spas, and other gimmicks.

PUBLIC HEALTH DISEASE NUMBER ONE

In 2013, Dr. Barry Solof wrote a text on Addiction Medicine for Therapists. In the preface, a section was entitled Closing The Gap Between Science and Medicine. Based upon a five-year national study by the National Center on Addiction and Substance Abuse at Columbia University (CASA Columbia), Solof pointed out considerable evidence to demonstrate the "neglect by the medical profession" in treating alcohol and other substance use diseases. He illustrated how "addiction treatment is largely disconnected from mainstream medicine", and that addiction treatment facilities and programs are not adequately regulated and held accountable.

Most existing treatment providers are staffed by people who are not required to have any medical training. Solof wrote that of all of the recent and necessary science available to primary health care physicians to screen, intervene and initially treat and refer patients, utilizing these evidence-based practices, were "rarely employed." He quoted Susan Foster, CASA Columbia's vice-president, stating "there is simply no other disease where appropriate medical treatment is not provided by the healthcare system and where patients instead must turn to a broad range of practitioners largely exempt from medical standards.[61]

The 2012 CASA Columbia study indicated a medical failure in our nation to treat substance disease. Some of the evidence included in the Solof text pointed to "the profound gap between what we know about the disease…versus current health and medical practice. Over twelve years ago, the study findings were:

- Over 40 million Americans had a substance addiction, which is more Americans than have heart conditions, diabetes or cancer
- Another 80 million were at risk substance users
- Less than 10% who needed addiction treatment received any help and most received less than quality, evidence-based, best practices care.
- Mainstream doctors rarely screened for risky use or addiction signs but treated a long list of health problems from related accidents, heart and lung disease, unintended pregnancies, liver disease and other costly conditions.
- Less than 1 in 3 patients were ever questioned about their alcohol use by general medical providers. Less than 6% of all referrals to addiction treatment came from mainstream health professionals, like primary care doctors.

Over thirty percent of states did not require treatment counselors to be licensed or certified and forty percent required only a high school diploma or GED; just seven states required addiction counselors to have a bachelor's degree. Compare those to the extensive requirements of mainstream medical professionals who treat all other chronic diseases.

Addiction and risky use of alcohol and other legal drugs constituted the largest preventable and most costly health problems facing the US; misuse is responsible for 20% of all deaths in the US and causes or contributes to poverty, other medical conditions and a third of all hospital in-patient costs.

Well, that was the picture of medical care in 2012. Over a decade later, we should have made considerable progress in addressing our number one public health issue, but the news is disheartening! The entire situation involving quality care based upon our scientific information available to address this disease, and the involvement of mainstream medicine is more problematic today. The gap between the extent of the public problem and the ability of mainstream medical doctors and practices to intervene is widening not receiving the necessary attention of public health leaders and practitioners.

Just recently, January 3, 2025, the US Surgeon General called for alcohol drinks to carry warning labels alerting their increasing cancer risk.[62] Also recent governmental reports indicated the rates of legal substance use disorders and their misuse is steadily increasing in almost all demographics, ages and social groups. This is following a considerable rate increase of alcohol and other substance use during in the pandemic.

The relapse rates of individuals with or without treatment are also increasing, despite the fact that there are many more profitable treatment facilities operating without sufficient quality.

Most medical schools are still not adequately preparing their graduates to deal with substance use disorders. This is a crime of negligence.

Recent studies have clearly demonstrated the hesitancy, even refusal by health systems and mainstream medical doctors to even screen their own patients for legal substance misuse. And we know about the epidemic of overdoses and deaths of young people from illegal drug use. What we don't read or hear much about is that human and financial consequences are steadily increasing with legal substance use and misuse.

As a society we now vote for, promote and desire an expanding spectrum of mind-altering substances to be easily available to us. Yet, we cannot seem to prepare our health systems to respond effectively to the harm that results from our appetite.

If we could just train our US primary care doctors to apply the evidence-based Screening, Brief Intervention and Referral To Treatment (SBIRT) tool to their existing patients and only refer individuals to treatment centers who are staffed properly, trained, regulated and accountable for quality, we could make a major stride toward slowing down the rates of addiction and relapses.

Doctors in mainstream medical practices in this country are used to using "norms" through hard data to treat or screen and refer to specialists other chronic, progressive and fatal (if untreated) diseases like cancer, heart disease, Parkinson's, diabetes and others. All we are asking is for them to do the same screening with substance use disorders.

OUR ALCOHOL DRIVEN CULTURE

Alcohol reaches the American consumer in many forms, via many processes and in many shapes, blends, colors, sizes, and containers. Our country is blanketed in a drinking culture that permeates most aspects of our life. The public advertising of drink is relentless and focused on almost all segments of the population. We have seltzers and wines for the dainty, high-powered craft beers for the stout, ice cold beer for the cool people, and various hard liquor for the rugged and adventurous. We have booze for real men camping on mountain cliffs and sparkling spritzers for elegant women. All legal, all business, all huge government tax revenues! Now college sources of income depend on alcohol sales. And accessibility to booze in grocery stores and gas stations is old news!

This is all good except that approximately one in seven people who drink with an alcohol use disorder, the additional cadre of binge drinkers, and the many who suffer harm or die from overconsumption by themselves or someone else.

Oh, I forgot! We are to drink responsibly! And when has any problem or heavy drinker consistently consumed booze responsibly? For certain, one in seven do not. Yet accessibility to alcohol is expanding and so is its public acceptability…until the drinker becomes sick enough to be ostracized for "becoming a problem or a drunk." Then if the shamed drinking person seeks help, he or she is expected to take on the stigma and become anonymous to find the right understanding, knowledge, and care needed. The drinking culture we have here in the US is not conducive to preventing and treating the disease of addiction that is widespread and growing.

The sad dichotomy underneath massive public and private support for the American drinking culture is that the public hypocritically shames the alcoholic or addict so much that the largest organization in the world, whose mission is to help, has to have its members continue to practice anonymity. This is still an unfortunate necessity to keep an individual identity secret in an attempt to reduce personal castigation and avoid the public shame of the disease.

AA's anonymity requirement dates back to 1935, when AA began in the climate of a public "moral model setting." It does not begin to synchronize with modern science's knowledge and today's "medical disease model." However, with our cultural norm of misinformed stigma, it remains a requisite for many programs. Sometimes I wonder what would happen to public perception if the millions of people around the world in recovery would come out of their closet and announce they are recovering from or being treated for a chronic, progressive, and fatal if untreated disease.

We don't have Diabetes Anonymous, Parkinson's Anonymous, Asthma Anonymous, Cancer or Heart Disease Anonymous. But because of the still present societal bias toward the disease of addiction, the necessity remains to maintain the anonymity of the other members of Alcoholics Anonymous. This necessary privacy, in turn, tends to reinforce the public shame, as well as the dangerous misconception that a substance use disorder rests with the willpower or character of the person. Clearly the scientific evidence gathered in the last twenty years proves "the moral model" of alcoholism (the willpower myth) is unquestionably erroneous and very harmful to the accessibility of treatment options for people suffering from the disease of a substance use disorder.

Another example of our societal hypocrisy with alcohol consumption is having people who are successfully in recovery describe being rejected or dismissed by an employer from a job because of their disease, even in remission. An individual who is in recovery and is honest about their disease is, to me, a far better risk to perform well on a job than those already in a company who are actively drinking heavily, whether secretly or outwardly.

So far, the public is generally not enlightened about alcoholism and prefers to blame who or what they don't understand. It's the old self-illusion that pointing out somebody else's problem makes me appear stronger. Ironically our "party and drug" culture mainly turns its back on individuals with alcohol or drug issues. Yet, as a society we are now opening legal access to cannabis, and possibly even hallucinogens. The door to legality continues to swing open for mind-altering substances because of the endless possibilities for the profits of "addiction capitalism'" and political gain. And at whose expense?

THE PUBLIC BIAS: "GOOD DRUGS" AND "BAD DRUGS"

In our society, use of alcohol, tobacco, and now marijuana, as well as a wide variety of prescription drugs, is legal, widely available, and heavily promoted. Therefore, drinking and other legal drug intake is commonly accepted in our culture, unlike say, heroin use. We generally consider drugs sold over the counter or legally prescribed (i.e., alcohol, nicotine, pain-killing opioids, sedatives and sleep meds, cannabis products, stimulants like Ritalin, and other commercial substances) as "good drugs." Often the exact same type of mind-altering chemicals sold illegally on the street or over the internet or are considered "bad drugs."

In this country a number of mind-altering substances are legal but highly addictive and very dangerous. What you will find out in this handbook is that all drugs, no matter their chemical effect, legal status, or how they are obtained, follow the same general pattern of interaction when entering the brain.

There is an initial neurological effect created by an introduced chemical. Following that, the brain adapts to counterbalance the effect of the drug. And then, with continued use of the mind-altering substance or substances, damaging neurological consequences occur, causing dysfunction.

US CULTURE AND ALCOHOL INTRINSICALLY WOVEN TOGETHER

In the US, alcohol has a very high level of cultural acceptance, an almost unlimited availability, and is constantly mass marketed. An enormous amount of media promotion is intended to initiate a cue-induced stimulation to drink. At certain times and places in our culture, opting not to drink or celebrate with alcohol is often chastised; at times it's considered unsociable. Often an awkward explanation for declining a drink is required.

In many social settings, especially for young people, proving themselves by the frequency or extensive amount they can drink or use another drug is a rite of passage. The vast majority of American entertainment, e.g., concerts and sporting events, promote and condone the use of alcohol and other drugs.

With its highly addictive nature and its misuse history of the drug as well as its legality, its accessibility, and our cultural norm of publicly promoting its use, alcohol is the most overused, abused, and damage-causing drug consumed in the United States. People with alcohol use disorder (AUD) are hardly attractive candidates for a harm-reduction approach involving the so-called "control" method of "responsible" drinking.

HARM REDUCTION AND THE MYTH OF "CONTROLLED DRINKING"

We support most but not all applications of what is a relatively ancient, but revived concept called harm reduction. Such "first do no harm" efforts are being generated to establish safety measures for substance users in order to prevent further harm or pain to them or others. Harm-reduction approaches can include medically weaning addicts off certain types of drug use by substituting the more dangerous substance use with a medically prescribed and properly monitored drug.

Harm reduction includes such measures as providing free clean needles to addicts in order to reduce the spread of illness. It can also include setting up accessible, public locations for obtaining a free drug such as Narcan to treat overdoses. No doubt, harm reduction is essential in many areas of addiction care, especially with opiate addicts. The challenge with harm-reduction strategies is to simultaneously ensure there are steps in place that protect public safety.

A number of harm-reduction strategies are successful in saving lives, decreasing relapse rates, and reducing crime associated with use of the more dangerous substances.[63] However, as it applies to alcohol use, a harm-reduction strategy of "controlled drinking" remains unproven on any sufficient scale. We consider it a hazardous strategy for individuals with an alcohol use disorder.

In addition, employing a "drug substitution" strategy is unadvisable. A considerable number of individuals who put down or cut down on their alcohol use for a temporary period of time will often substitute their drug of choice, say alcohol, with another replacement substance like marijuana or painkillers. This does not constitute what we consider true sobriety.

ADDICTION CARE PROBLEMS IN THE CURRENT PUBLIC HEALTH SYSTEM

In this country, our primary health problems related to substance use disorder involve the extent and growth of the disease; the lack of knowledge, attention, and resources to prevent and treat the disease effectively for a lifetime; and the vast resources, financial and human, being wasted on our misguided penal approach and ineffective disease care.

The practice of screening for alcohol use disorder and other substance use disorders by American mainstream physicians is at least twenty years behind the science.

Adding to this knowledge deficiency in addiction medicine and care is the shortage of American health care professionals in general and also specifically in addiction medicine. There are a variety of reasons for the deficiency, including relative lower income potential, misunderstandings and biases about the disease model itself, and the perceived difficulty of the potential stereotypical clientele.

Furthermore the shortage of personnel in the addiction field itself, far too many general or family practice physicians who are on the medical frontline (where addiction assessment, diagnosis, and treatment should commonly be initiated) are either hesitant, unable, or unwilling to deal with the initial screening and intervention of an addiction disorder.

For most people with the disease of substance use, being referred to a quality treatment center by their family doctor, let alone being admitted to a quality treatment program with an adequate follow-up protocol for a sufficient time, are both highly improbable. Even emergency care doctors, who are often on the front line of care for alcohol use and substance use cases, are reluctant to screen and refer these patients for immediate and appropriate help.

It might be revealing to examine the number of criminal justice employees paid for by the public in this country, or to total the public expenditures of our local, state, and national governments used to investigate, arrest, prosecute, try, incarcerate, house, feed, guard, medically treat, release, and implement the probation of addiction-related, nonviolent (often repeat) offenders.

It would be equally enlightening to compare the total of US public justice system expenditures for nonviolent alcohol- and drug-related offenders in our nation with the total expenditures of our public funding for establishing properly trained addiction doctor specialists, nurses, counselors, and other medical support staff involved in diagnosis, treatment, and follow-up care of the chronic, progressive disease called substance use disorder. The comparison of the total cost of providing "criminal justice" versus providing "addiction disease medical care" in this country is staggeringly one-sided.

It blows my mind to think of how much money (in the trillions of dollars) has been spent and how many lives have and continue to be wasted in the name of justice. How many people's lives and families are being further damaged because we refuse to treat addiction as a disease and not a crime?

Perhaps we feel safer locking up people with a chronic disease, but we aren't safer. Perhaps it helps us to feel morally superior to "others" with obvious addictions. Perhaps, we remain ignorant of the disease and still stigmatized by past misconceptions, just simply ignorant of the basic science of addiction. Or, in this day and age, perhaps we believe we know more than science, can disregard science to fit our own preconceived narrative.

The real shame is not in having a chronic addiction disease. The real shame is the human suffering that continues to be unnecessarily inflicted on diseased people, their families, and their communities. In a recent national study, over 40 percent of US citizens are familiar with a person who has died from a drug overdose. I'm guessing nearly all of us know someone who has what we suspect to be a drinking or "using" (legal or illegal drug) problem. I'm certain we also know families being torn apart by the consequences and premature deaths from alcohol and substance use.

"If the jailer goes home, the prisoner is freed"! The disease and those who use it to punish the truly sick are, in addition to the addicted souls, also the jailers. Only the effectively treated are free. Our family has so far been freed from the bondage that accompanies the disease. We were very lucky, so fortunate that one of the few quality recovery programs in Ohio at that time just happened to be located in the backyard of our hometown.

The story of our family history with its substance addiction and recovery is the rarity, an outlier, a jewel, a treasure of blessings granted to us by grace. Our family story has somehow woven its way through the depths of a tragic spiral of fear and despair and suffering. But eventually a transformation appeared in the darkness. The horrors of a disease that progressively imprisons the mind, body, and soul have morphed into an uplifting tale of hope and faith and gratitude and freedom and, above all, a love story! Many suffering individuals with a substance use disorder and their families don't fare as well. But recovery "will work if you seek it, find it, and work it!"

One of my executive board members once told me that "for positive transformational change to occur with anything, you need the right idea, the right people, the right place, and the right time to come together." In our family experience with substance addiction, this synchronicity somehow miraculously appeared.

We didn't earn or deserve the positive transformation from sickness to health any more than any others tortured with this disease. Our family, unlike many other addiction-afflicted individuals and families, happened to discover our need for professional help, and there were recovery support Champions readily available to help us. The rest of the story has been a positive, redemptive history . . . so far.

THE MERRY-GO-ROUND IN THE WILD WEST OF "REHAB"

I've heard the current state of addiction care in this country aptly described as "the Wild West of Rehab." With mainstream medical practices providing largely undirected or general referrals into the land of unregulated "rehab care," this current hodgepodge referral practice most often fails to follow up and monitor the progress of the person with a relapsing chronic disease.

Short-term, often corner-cutting treatment and little follow-up care or support don't cut it! The result is a continuing "merry-go-round" of wasted dollars, brief treatment attempts, repetitive relapses, and countless destroyed lives and families.

As the merry-go-round continues, most of our public officials and community health systems, our primary medical practices and professionals, our academic institutions, and many medical schools remain stuck in a status quo model of scarcity, omission, and unfortunately, ignorance. For example, check out the present number of classes and the amount of curriculum offered at your nearest medical or nursing school currently targeted toward addiction medicine and best practices of care! Not many, considering the extent of harm experienced by the consequences of substance use disorders.

The state of Ohio, like other states that won large legal financial settlements from opioid manufacturers, is presently awarding millions of dollars from their settlement fund. They are doing so with good intentions, funding "projects" and "programs" scattered throughout political regions around the state from over a thousand plus applications.

A significant amount of "recovery foundation" money could be used to implement the ground floor for a statewide system of effective addiction community care in Ohio with established standards of quality, performance, and accountability. Such a transformation would provide the foundation for far more significant long-term benefits in better addiction care statewide for many more people and many years to come. Funding siloed rehabs and individual "programs" without a quality standards and true regulatory enforcement in place pushes us further away from a regulated, measurable, accountable system. Right now, nearly anyone can publicly advertise they are operating a successful facility or program. Hanging a shingle or setting up a nicely designed website to attract desperate silent sufferers is simple. Providing quality treatment is a whole different proposition.

A recent article in the *Palm Beach Post* entitled "The Florida Shuffle," written by Antigone Barton, exposes the all-too-familiar failures of a state that allows—even promotes—a "corrupt economy that makes failed treatment more profitable than recovery."[64]

According to the article, the Florida state agency responsible for "an industry notorious for fraud, negligence and abuse," provides little oversight, and its monitoring of programs in the state is dysfunctional. Allegedly, the agency assigned to the addiction care oversight in Florida has little expertise in health care, let alone addiction prevention and medicine.

The state of Florida is accused of not holding facilities to evidence-based standards of care or ensuring patient safety. They allegedly have not appropriately managed patient or provider records, and they allegedly have allowed a lack of response to reported violations of conduct. The state is also charged with negligence in issuing and renewing licenses to allow facilities to operate without meeting even the basics of any quality assurance indicators. I believe this is the case in many states. Performance in every other medical field is important. Why not substance disorders, which are chronic diseases of the brain and body?

One of the most pertinent criticisms of "The Florida Shuffle" rehabs is that few of the medical directors of treatment programs in the state have the credentials or experience in the necessary specialties of addiction medicine and psychiatry. Nor are they available on site. What about the other staff members? How many of them are properly trained and licensed in the field of addiction medicine and counseling?

We are aware of other states with treatment programs that have similar deficiencies to Florida in their professional and performance system oversight. There is an obvious lack of monitoring of "rehabs" and "programs" operating under the radar of many states. The online marketing of these Wild West programs is often unsurprisingly state-of-the-art, their program enrollment instantly accessible, and of course, their operation is financially profitable for poor quality, usually short-term treatment.

Now that young people can legally remain on their parents' insurance longer and insurance providers are legally required to cover addiction care, "treatment" is popping up everywhere. So are relapse rates! But at what cost?

An ineffective care environment amounts to isolated, short-term, or unaccountable efforts that appear reasonable on the surface. Who is measuring processes and results when funds are handed out in your state? Better yet, who maintains consistent performance data on providers, showing chronic care results that deserve public funding *before* it's handed out?

We are encouraging states to implement broad systemic changes using the best clinical and infrastructure strategies and practices already available. This includes involvement of mainstream medical practices; the creation/monitoring/auditing standards of provider care; the establishment of performance measurement data systems with public transparency of reporting results specific to substance use disorder care.

Often these elements are not incorporated into state treatment and recovery planning. Thus, the "siloed" system of the status quo continues with the overall addiction care system wasting dollars and lives.

There is an absence of an addiction care system with a congruent, cohesive and professional environment in which to operate. Until a public medical professional care system emerges, the shadow of addiction care will not be lifted. The silence and shame will continue to flourish in the "silo" of darkness, the absence of light!

A new system of quality care and treatment needs to be channeled through the entry point of existing mainstream primary care practices as the primary entry point of service, then to other quality-demonstrated treatment providers and support groups. Peer recovery coaching, extended patient monitoring, telemedicine, online disease education, and patient progress rewards are additional elements of a more effective care system that have been proven to be best practices as well.

CAUTION ABOUT THE QUALITY OF RECOVERY TREATMENT, UNPROVEN IDEAS AND UNDOCUMENTED PROGRAMS

When you see the term *evidence-based* used to describe a miracle cure or read an article or teaser about a new gimmicky recovery method, investigate before believing. We are aware of several instances in the history of alcoholism when isolated or random studies have been selectively used to substantiate desired conclusions. To investigate research in the field of addiction, we recommend verifying the extent, methodology, quantity, and very importantly, the acceptance of specific findings by the broader addiction or neurological expert community.

The Centers for Disease Control and Prevention (CDC) categorizes research in the field as either "well-supported," "supported," or "promising." For example, the characterization of substance addiction as a chronic disease is well-supported, but not the idea of "controlled drinking."

A month-long period of abstinence called "Dry January," or a reduced-drinking monthly stretch like "Damp January" may have some temporary health benefits, such as lower blood pressure, less cancer or heart disease risk, and the improvement of your mental health or liver function.

Trying not to drink for a month, or drinking on a reduced frequency, and failing to meet either of these "control" goals is also a significant indicator that you do not have a realistic perspective of your own habit. I went without drinking for one or more months on several occasions. Then I went weeks, then days, then hours! Of course, I mentally used such abstinences as proof to myself that I was, I surmised, still in control of my drinking. It was just another self-deceiving rationalization that led me to binge drink—and increasingly more over the damaging years.

BEHAVIORAL COUNSELING NOT THE BEST STARTING PLACE FOR TREATMENT OF A SUBSTANCE USE DISORDER (SUD)

Cognitive Behavioral Therapy (CBT), Family Systems Counseling, and other forms of psychological counseling are extremely important treatment tools that help many people with addiction, especially those receiving a dual diagnosis with SUD in combination with another co-occurring psychiatric disorder. However, only after the basic physiological issues are assessed and treatment initiated (e.g., detox) should behavioral or other psychological therapy initiatives be considered. The dysfunctional brain needs to clear some first before new learning can occur effectively.

The daily process of *unlearning* and *relearning* required in initial recovery depends upon a degree of mental clarity and pain relief before the new experience of changing thoughts, responses, and behavioral modifications can occur effectively. Relearning is a continuous and essential requirement for initiating and maintaining recovery. Simply stated, the brain and body need time (sometimes weeks or months) to lessen the dysfunction of brain fog before a person can mentally, emotionally, or habitually adjust, especially in an acute or even prolonged withdrawal state.

WORDS MATTER!

It is also helpful to use language that supports the disease model while eliminating words that continue to reinforce the stigma of the moral model. Words matter; they carry connotations! Seeing alcohol or drug addiction as a substance use disorder, a primary and progressive and chronic disease, can begin to erase stigma.

Which specific drugs do our society and our government value or legally allow and promote? What language does society commonly use to describe the real disease nature of our nation's greatest public health problem. How do certain words reflect our collective knowledge levels and our perspective of the addiction issue's significance? Especially how and with what resolve have we confronted the matter?

The use of consistent, non-stigmatizing language, medical terminology and references to the disease nature of substance addiction are vital to eliminating widespread societal barriers to caring appropriately for addicted people and their families. The current levels of moral judgment, misinformation, and shaming stigma impede adequate treatment of addiction in our nation. Simultaneously, a combination of societal ignorance of science and subsequent governmental policy is responsible for a still burgeoning criminal justice system that unnecessarily and ineffectively imprisons millions of nonviolent addicted people, at unfathomably staggering costs.

THE MODERN MEDICAL DISEASE MODEL OF TREATMENT FOR PATIENTS AND FAMILIES

Fortunately, in our nation we do have some medical providers currently using the "modern disease model" to treat substance use disorder patients with quality and integrity.

Model addiction treatment programs have supportive medical, psychological, and social services, as well as physical exercise activities and family education programs. These pioneers of community recovery are program role models that utilize the best practice diagnosis and treatment criteria and practice regimens recommended by The American Society of Addiction Medicine (ASAM). Also, these models, which include monitoring protocols for aftercare and longer-term follow-up, are an essential element for the care of chronic diseases.

Also of note, Medical-Assisted Treatment (MAT) for addiction is gaining by leaps and bounds. According to a recent worldwide study. MAT is a corollary to the twelve-step methodology of recovery and has proven itself as very effective in helping those in early recovery avoid relapse.

AN EXAMPLE OF A QUALITY CARE TREATMENT FACILITY

Several of us contributing to these handbooks formerly spent time together at the Shepherd Hill Behavioral Health Campus of the Licking Memorial Health Systems (LMHS) in Newark, Ohio. Dr. Richard Whitney was the Medical Director, Dr. Wendy Talbott Flowers, the Family Education Program Coordinator, and I gave weekly patient lectures with "Coach's Corner" discussions.

The "Hill" (as the Shepherd Hill Behavioral Health campus is called locally) has been one of the exemplary centers in the addiction field beginning with the leadership of local physician Dr. William Kennedy in 1983. Forty years of experience at the "Hill" equates to a lot of recovered lives and families!

The Shepherd Hill Campus is a facility that uses a comprehensive recovery model. The Hill offers quality assessment, diagnosis, treatment, associated medical services, highly trained and experienced staff, aftercare, community recovery group integration, and family education regarding substance use disorder.

At Shepherd Hill the medical director is a full-time, on-campus doctor, specifically trained as an addiction specialist practicing the modern medical treatment model. Psychiatrists, psychologists, trained addiction and family counselors, nurses, social workers, and trained aides are also available onsite.

Combined with daily education sessions, group therapy, and individual medical and counseling appointments, patients are connected with a range of other medical and mental health sources. Many other community resources and support, including transportation to daily twelve-step group meetings and physical wellness activities, housing assistance, and employment services are made available to program patients. The

Shepherd Hill Campus is not a fancy resort facility with spas and horseback riding stables. It does, however, offer the required basics of proven best practices for clinical care.

The issue is how to replicate the few quality programs that exist in Ohio and make them more available, accessible, and affordable to individuals and families—quality recovery centers like Shepherd Hill in Newark, the Ridges near Cincinnati, Ohio Ridges now in the north Columbus (Polaris) area or Glenbeigh near Cleveland. The challenge is creating more top-level, full-service treatment and chronic care management availability and accessibility for middle-class and working-class people in more locations.

I am very partial to the program design and qualified staff at Shepherd Hill after my daughter's recovery following her lengthy stay there several decades ago. To say that Shepherd Hill was instrumental in saving our daughter's life is not an exaggeration.

A major problem facing Shepherd Hill and other high quality, disease model treatment centers is that the majority of operational funding available to them from a few outside sources like the government or private insurance companies can be limited, complex, and confusing. The coding bureaucracy attached to public and private insurers is mind-boggling, inefficient, and unnecessarily costly. Enrollment into treatment can be a major barrier for people and a roadblock for providers.

An extreme shortage exists in our area of top-tier treatment programs to truly meet the potential demand for care and simultaneously lower relapse rates significantly.

Consequently:

- Many individuals don't go anywhere; few are aware of or try twelve-step groups directly
- Most individuals go to inadequate treatment places that cut corners
- Many individuals exhaust funds going to short-term, but don't have resources for coaching, monitoring support and necessary follow-up care
- A few individuals get lucky and eventually find the help they need on their own

95 percent of individuals with a substance use disorder never get any help, and the limited number who do get treatment experience high relapse rates.

Another practice that occurs in some treatment programs is in their admissions process, when they will sometimes diagnose a substance disorder patient with other mental health issues for advantageous fee and billing purposes. In these cases, patient confusion about their diagnosis often interferes with the actual substance disease treatment.

I have had several therapists suggest to me that traditional counseling was what I needed, and my alcohol intake would resolve itself. I've had ministers suggest the church would help take away my desire for alcohol. While I firmly support behavioral health as well as a strong spiritual life, neither are as effective without addressing my primary, physiological, progressive, chronic disease. A good counselor or pastor needs to know this.

Recovery from a substance use disorder is no different in scope and length than treating heart disease. I may pray, I may consult with a heart fitness expert, but nothing is better than a great cardiologist answering my prayers. Get the right addiction medicine doctor first for substance disease! Then do the work that recovery requires. If that work involves psychological or pastoral counseling, all the better, after the brain has cleared some!

Without question, a total paradigm shift in public policy regarding addiction treatment and criminal justice is needed. Primarily our American middle class deserves a new, more effective, available, and successful public health and insurance business model to treat the disease of substance use disorder. Today's public addiction policy is akin to placing a Band-Aid on a cancer lesion!

GRATITUDE FOR MIRACLES

Our family can unequivocally attest that the original three-month, inpatient, residential treatment at Shepherd Hill for our child has been the foundation for a long-term remission of the disease. The treatment at her young age resulted in a most worthwhile, long-term investment. At the time, twenty-five years ago, the likelihood of a possible positive outcome for our college student entering treatment was anything but assured. Looking back, by grace, our family has been granted many blessings of recovery.

At that same period of time, the Shepherd Hill staff also indirectly influenced my own pathway to recovery. For my wife, the family program at Shepherd Hill motivated her lifelong involvement in the Al-Anon 12 step support group for individual spouses, family members and friends who have problem drinkers and users in their lives. The initial struggle for our daughter to obtain quality treatment at age twenty has become the gift that has kept on giving!

Addiction is a family disease. Our initial experience of chaos has been transformed to one of learning, hope and joy!

Summarizing, when an individual achieves long-term recovery from this disease, it often involves the following:

- A personal recognition of the need for help
- Family/friend support
- Immediate accessibility to qualified medical help
- Initial screening, brief intervention and if needed, further medical care
- Immediate access to quality assessment, diagnosis, and treatment
- Financial resources arrangements and navigation assistance
- An individualized treatment plan
- Sufficient time in quality treatment with qualified addiction medical professionals
- Early integration into community recovery groups

- Early integration of family members and close friends into disease education and family support programs
- Aftercare, long-term monitoring, and addiction coaching
- An individual relapse prevention and relapse plan
- Total abstinence from alcohol and other addictive substances not in the individual treatment plan, and under professional supervision and monitoring
- Continuing education about the disease with guided behavioral change and an emphasis on a daily path of spiritual steps and growth
- Long-term involvement in a community recovery support group

RECOVERY REQUIREMENT: DAILY FUNDAMENTAL PRACTICE

- Most importantly, we want to emphasize that recovery from a chronic disease requires daily habit formation and strengthening, as well as chronic care management and monitoring. Recovery is "one day at a time" for a lifetime. The daily process of *unlearning and relearning* is required to neurologically rewire the brain's neural pathways. This brain rewiring leads to more healthy thoughts and positive behavioral responses and fewer stressful consequences.
- A sense of serenity is best achieved with consistent daily recovery practices within a team environment of trusted support. The winning "team culture" is formed by individuals who have directly experienced addiction and are on the "recovery squad" facing the same chronic disease opponent of substance addiction.
- I share with newcomers in recovery that I could study videos of NBA legend LeBron James all day long and pick up good ideas on how to be a great basketball player, but unless I (attend) practice consistently, I won't (a) improve my individual skills or (b) learn to fit my own skills into a coordinated and supportive team concept when going against a tough opponent. For me, the toughest opponent I face every day is substance addiction. LeBron has a lot of answers on the court. But for what we are dealing with, facing this life-or-death opponent of substance addiction requires a whole new level of long-term learning, skill development through daily fundamental practice, and teamwork with peers!

A TEAM OF CHAMPIONS

- The chronic disease opponent of substance addiction never disappears! Isolation and loneliness are highly dangerous to someone trying to get sober and healthy. For the silent sufferer of a substance disorder, the best longer-term strategy for finding and maintaining a healthy recovery is to be active

daily on a team of recovering peers with a single, shared purpose: to become physically, mentally, and spiritually well.
- I refer to all people, including families who support recovery programs as "Champions", because in some direct way, they are facing and opposing a most dangerous, life-threatening opponent every day. Involvement in any form of support for recovering individuals and recovery groups deserves Champion status.
- One of the first things you are told to do when you attend a group recovery program is to hang with the "Winners": those who attend "Recovery Practice" (team meetings) regularly and visibly demonstrate "progress with principles" (fundamental guiding skills).
- It is extremely beneficial to be regularly engaged with people who are successfully recovering from addiction. They are most likely able and willing to help us neutralize our mutual disease "Opponent" that is commonly shared. Nobody understands a person with a substance addiction better than a "Teammate" with the same neurological disease and sobriety/recovery objective. We subscribe to the axiom that "a problem shared is a problem halved."
- In our organizational framework, recovery accompanied by a collective team is so vital. In addition to those of us with the disorder, the team also includes our family members, friends, and other supportive individuals who become educated about substance use disorders and are working with us to promote positive collaborative care for those battling with the disease.
- Aside from early integration into existing twelve-step or other community groups, we strongly encourage utilizing peer recovery support or addiction coaching teams that are certified or licensed. These patient prevention, education and treatment support teams can be a tremendous asset to community care efforts (1) in the outreach assistance to new patients identified by mainstream medical screenings, (2) in the extended encouragement, support, education, and monitoring of patients leaving treatment, and (3) in community care resource development.
- Based upon proven longer term, patient monitoring models that have demonstrated much lower relapse rates, and consequently reduced costs, we recommend at least two years of regular patient support as a success-driven supplement to quality treatment.
- To address substance use disorder, we endorse first obtaining early screening, and, if necessary, receiving initial medical treatment and a referral for early integration into a recovery group. By affiliation with individuals who are in recovery, regular connection to positive influences with experience confronting the disease serves as the reinforcement for effective recovery practices. Connection with other recovering teammates also establishes a critical point of mutual accountability and commitment beyond the capacity of a single person's good intentions or willpower.
- To keep the disease from returning—to "stay stopped" by avoiding relapse and more damage—the important initial care plan needs to be managed via vital long-term monitoring to ensure the proper

assessment, treatment, and referrals are implemented. This longer-term strategy centers on executing a new and active daily routine of attending recovery "practice" with new Teammates.

THE ROOMS OF SHOCK AND AWE

Recovery Is Gospel (Good News). To recover from a substance use disorder, old (thoughts, emotional responses, habits, behaviors) are eased out! New is eased in! Alcohol or substance addiction doesn't develop overnight, and so recovery is not instantaneous either. It takes time and care and connection. However, the good news is the bad news isn't true! It's not about bad people getting good. It's about sick folks getting well. Time, positive examples, collaborative care/support, and a safe environment are key to receiving the good news of recovery.

- Hope is found "in the rooms" where the groups (Teams) of recovery programs meet to share their mutual experiences, strengths, and hopes. I remember when I first attended a recovery team meeting (Practice), I was shocked at the different types of people there, some of whom looked very familiar. How welcoming they were to me and how much laughter prevailed in the rooms. I was also in awe of how familiar I was with the nature of their discussion and how I related to so much of what was read and said.
- Trying to recover from a substance disorder in isolation is most often futile. Even if someone stops drinking on their own, there are real benefits of a proven recovery program beyond sobriety, which are in the program's continuing community of daily support and its repetitive methods leading to positive behavioral and relationship changes. The essential need of a real recovery is more than just stopping drinking or stopping use of a substance.
- Recovery is about changing the way we live life and becomes associated with healthy ideas, people, places, things, and events. Recovery is not about entering a lengthy isolation from reality and the outside world. In essence, recovery is relearning to live successfully with yourself and others while accepting the realties of real life.
- Recovery from alcohol or other drug disorders isn't a ticket to Utopia, a perfect world without difficulty. You are not in real recovery if you just stop drinking or using, but still exhibit being a "dry drunk" with behaviors of anger, irritability, and discontentment.
- Returning to the same unhealthy environment in which your addiction or its associated negative behaviors are stimulated by certain cues, individuals, locations, ideas, items, senses, or events, is a surefire way to reignite your illness and guarantee your relapse. A key relearning area in recovery is how to recognize and reject cues or triggers.

"HALF-MEASURES AVAILED US NOTHING"

The ability to maintain a "dry" month like Dry January or a "damp" period is not anywhere close to an effective recovery treatment for the disease itself. However, if you are tempted to try such "half measures" (as they are known in the recovery community), this in itself likely indicates you at least might have the suspicion of an out-of-control problem with drinking and probably need to look for some help.

Trying half measures is a subtle way an addicted person internally or subconsciously privately admits to themselves a silent concern about their own drinking or drugging, but without wanting to seriously consider giving up the substance use. How else would it be possible to feel good or feel normal or feel anything again?

A common fear of a problem drinker is what we would do with ourselves without potential occasions to drink. We project how boring life would be or how we would not enjoy any relaxation time without booze or a mind-altering substance. This type of projection and rationalization is very commonplace, but it is so misleading and dangerous.

I read an article titled "Don't Quit Booze, Just Drink Differently," quoting the CEO of an outfit called Alcohol Change UK. In the article the author asserts that "he used to be a heavy drinker." He says he wants to encourage a sense of experimentation in January with drinking. He professes that alcohol is optional for him, while he still loves going to bars. Whoa![65]

The author, I am sure, has good intentions, but my guess is, had I accepted the moderating claim of his message to "control my drinking" on the day before I became aware and admitted my own desperation to stop twenty-five years ago, I might possibly have found just enough false hope in his tempting idea to avoid quitting entirely. Were that the case, I would have likely been dead or institutionalized by now. It is so easy as an addicted or "heavy" drinker to deceive ourselves into trying an easier, softer way to reduce our drinking consequences. When we do this, we reenter the typical state of denial, the strongest defense mechanism for a person with an alcohol or other substance use disorder.

"DON'T THINK"

When I desperately returned to a recovery program after years of active drinking, because I had "thought" I was thinking rationally and clearly, the first thing Ben, my new program sponsor, told me to do was, ironically, "Don't Think!" When I began to question that counterintuitive thought, Ben said, "Look pal, your best thinking brought you here in the toxic state you are in! Analysis paralysis! When you are in your head for any length of time, you are behind enemy lines, especially in early sobriety. So put a plug in the jug, pull the cotton out of your ears, and try listening for a while. Will you please quit wasting time thinking about the failed illusions you have been carrying around!" In other words, Ben was encouraging me to "relearn" how I was trying to live my life while depending upon my alcohol intake as the crutch for my dysfunctional thinking. "Stinkin' thinking" he called it. Then, I can still hear him reminding me, "Aren't you aware it was your thinking that led to your drinking that brought you here looking for answers in the first place!" He taught me, "When the student is ready, the rabbi appears!"

Unfortunately, what amounts to the most welcomed self-deceit for a drinker, to moderate or control alcohol intake is undeniably the primary reason the relapse rate of this chronic disease is so high. The ability for individuals with a substance use disorder to fool themselves into searching for the magic bullet, the illusion to control the uncontrollable, is why substance addiction is labeled "cunning, baffling and powerful."

Anyone who suggests a method "to think your way out of drinking" is selling the snake oil of wishful thinking. This type of rational or cerebral effort opposes the recent neurological evidence of a chronic brain and body disorder. It minimizes the powerful effects of substance withdrawal and the craving stages of the disease when not drinking or using.

Leading a person who misuses alcohol in the first place to believe they can control their drinking, encouraging them to experiment with alcohol intake, or suggesting someone just hang out in bars where alcohol flows, is not my idea of prudence or even common sense. The chances of a problem or binge drinker trying these "against-the-odds" temptations and escaping harmful drinking consequences for very long are prohibitive. Being an arsonist and playing harmlessly with fire doesn't work. The neurological science and experiential data fail to support this appealing but dangerously erroneous "controlled experimentation to drinking happiness" theory.

ASK THE TEAM DOC

With RICHARD N. WHITNEY, MD, DABAM, FASAM

When serving as the medical director at Shepherd Hill, Dr. Whitney conducted an hour-long session called "Ask the Doc" at the weekly Saturday morning family program. Here we share with you questions often asked by new treatment patients and their family members, and his responses.

QUESTION 1: Do you consider alcohol or drug addiction to be a medical disease? If so, why?

ANSWER: Many people don't understand why or how other people become addicted to drugs. They may mistakenly think that those who use drugs lack moral principles or willpower—that they could stop their drugs use simply by choosing to. In reality, drug addiction is a complex disease, and quitting usually takes more than good intentions or a strong will. Drugs change the brain in ways that make quitting hard, even for those who want to. Fortunately, researchers know more than ever about how drugs affect the brain, and researchers have found treatments that can help people recover from drug addiction and lead productive lives.

QUESTION 2: What is drug addiction?

ANSWER: Addiction is a chronic disease characterized by drug seeking and use that is compulsive, or difficult to control, despite harmful consequences. The initial decision to take drugs is voluntary for most people, but repeated drug use can lead to brain changes that challenge an addicted person's self-control and interfere with their ability to resist intense urges to take drugs. These brain changes can be persistent, which is why drug addiction is considered a "relapsing" disease—people in recovery from drug use disorders are at increased risk for returning to drug use even after years of not taking the drug.

It's common for a person to relapse, but relapse doesn't mean that treatment doesn't work. As with other chronic health conditions, treatment should be ongoing and should be adjusted based on how the patient responds. Treatment plans need to be reviewed often and modified to fit the patient's changing needs.

Most addictive drugs affect the brain's "reward circuit," causing euphoria as well as flooding it with the chemical messenger dopamine. A properly functioning reward system motivates a person to repeat behaviors needed to thrive, such as eating and spending time with loved ones. Surges of dopamine in the reward circuit cause the reinforcement of pleasurable but unhealthy behaviors like taking drugs, leading people to repeat the behavior again and again.

As a person continues to use drugs, the brain adapts by reducing the ability of cells in the reward circuit to respond to it. This reduces the high that the person feels compared to the high they felt when first taking the drug—an effect known as tolerance. They might take more of the drug to try and achieve the same high. These brain adaptations often lead to the person becoming less and less able to derive pleasure from other things they once enjoyed, like food, sex, or social activities.

Long-term use also causes changes in other brain chemical systems and circuits as well, affecting functions that include:
- learning
- judgment
- decision-making
- stress
- memory
- behavior

Despite being aware of these harmful outcomes, many people who use drugs continue to take them, which is the nature of addiction.

QUESTION 3: How do I know if I have a problem with alcohol? Is there a test I could take privately?

ANSWER: Here are several diagnostic tools that are publicly available online:

1. DSM 5 Diagnostic Criteria
https://www.niaaa.nih.gov/sites/default/files/alcohol-symptom-checklist.pdf
Mild AUD is 2-3 symptoms, moderate AUD is 4-5 symptoms, and severe AUD is 6 or more symptoms.
2. Alcohol Use Disorders Identification Test
https://auditscreen.org/check-your-drinking/
3. NIAAA Single Alcohol Screening Question (SASQ)
"How many times in the past year have you had (4 for women, or 5 for men) or more drinks in a day?"
A response of *one or more* warrants follow-up.
What are the 4 CAGE test questions?

CAGE Alcohol Questionnaire
- Have you felt the need to Cut down on your drinking?
- Do you feel Annoyed by people complaining about your drinking?
- Do you ever feel Guilty about your drinking?
- Do you ever drink an Eye-opener in the morning to relive the shakes?

QUESTION 4: If drugs are legal in the marketplace or are prescribed by a licensed medical professional, aren't they less harmful than legal drugs people buy on the street?

ANSWER: https://nida.nih.gov/sites/default/files/rxreportfinalprint.pdf
This is a link to the NIH Research Report Series: Prescription Drug Abuse.

QUESTION 5: I don't think I have an alcohol issue. I only drink and may get wasted on weekends or holidays and vacations. I don't drink every day. So?

ANSWER: Although drinking any amount of alcohol can carry certain risks, crossing the binge threshold increases the risk of acute harm, such as blackouts and overdoses. Binge drinking also increases the likelihood of unsafe sexual behavior and the risk of sexually transmitted infections or unintentional pregnancy. These risks are greater at higher peak levels of consumption. Because of the impairments it produces, binge drinking also increases the likelihood of a host of potentially deadly consequences, including falls, burns, drownings, and car crashes.

Alcohol affects virtually all tissues in the body. Data suggests that even one episode of binge drinking can compromise the function of the immune system and lead to acute pancreatitis (inflammation of the pancreas) in individuals with underlying pancreatic damage. Over time, alcohol misuse, including repeating episodes of binge drinking, contributes to liver and other neck, esophageal, liver, breast, and colorectal cancers.

Binge drinking can be deadly. Approximately 140,000 deaths resulted from alcohol misuse annually in the United States between 2015 and 2019, and almost half of those were associated with binge drinking. Binge drinking is also costly.

QUESTION 6: How do you treat someone with an alcohol use or other substance use disorder who has severe chronic pain issues or severe anxiety?

ANSWER: There are multiple nonaddictive medications that can effectively treat mild, moderate, and severe chronic pain issues. These include nonsteroidal anti-inflammatory medications, acetaminophen, antiepileptic medications, and many others. Targeted injections (into joints or muscles or other body parts) are frequently used for pain control. Transcutaneous electrical nerve simulations (TENS) units may be helpful. Physical therapy, chiropractic care, and massage are frequently used for pain control. Various modalities of psychological therapy, including cognitive behavioral therapy (CBT), operant-behavioral therapy, mindfulness-based stress reduction, and acceptance and commitment therapy have all been found to be helpful as well.

Similarly, many nonaddictive medications and techniques are successfully used for relief of anxiety disorders. These may include medications such as beta-blockers, serotonin selective reuptake inhibitors (SSRIs), or serotonin-norepinephrine reuptake inhibitors (SNIRs), tricyclic antidepressant medications (TCAs), buspirone, major tranquilizers, and others. Additionally, various forms of psychotherapy may be very helpful for relief of anxiety disorders.

QUESTION 7: Marijuana and other assorted cannabis products are now legal in many states. Do you see a problem with their use?

ANSWER: Cannabis use has been shown to be associated with cognitive decline, impaired educational or occupational attainment, risk of other substance use disorders, and poor quality of life. It has also been shown to be associated with impaired driving and fatal vehicle crashes, cannabis-related emergency room visits, psychosis and psychiatric comorbidity.

Cannabis Use Disorder (CUD) has been associated with disability and strongly and consistently associated with other substance use and mental disorders. Use of high potency cannabis has been associated with increased frequency of use, cannabis use-related problems, and increased likelihood of anxiety disorder.

QUESTION 8: I have an alcohol problem, so I have stopped drinking altogether, and now relax by smoking a little grass. Isn't this a less problematic option for me?

ANSWER: (See Answer 7# above)

QUESTION 9: I am used to having a six pack or two daily after work. My counselor suggests that I limit myself to two beers or drinks and only three days a week. I know I drink far too much on a regular basis and am thinking about quitting cold turkey. Can't I do it myself, by myself?

ANSWER: Alcohol withdrawal is a disease syndrome with potentially serious consequences. Symptoms begin as early as six hours after the initial decline from peak intoxication. Initial symptoms include tremor, anxiety, insomnia, restlessness, and nausea. Particularly in mildly alcohol-dependent persons, these symptoms may compromise the entire disease syndrome and may subside without treatment after a few days.

More serious withdrawal symptoms occur in approximately ten percent of patients. These symptoms include a low-grade fever, rapid breathing, tremor, and profuse sweating. Seizures may occur in more than five percent of untreated patients in acute alcohol withdrawal.

Another severe complication is delirium tremens (DTs), which is characterized by hallucinations, mental confusion, and disorientation. The mortality rate among patients exhibiting DTs is 5 to 25 percent. It is best to check with a licensed healthcare professional regarding cessation of regular alcohol use.

QUESTION 10: Is substance addiction genetic?

ANSWER: More than half of the differences in how likely people are to develop substance use problems stem from DNA differences, though it varies a little bit by substance. Research suggests alcohol addiction is about 50 percent heritable, and addiction to certain other drugs can be more than 70 percent heritable.

QUESTION 12: I've heard people in my AA group say that medicine treatment forfeits my sobriety. What's your opinion/experience about these so-called "addiction meds"?

ANSWER: From "The A.A. Member — Medications and Other Drugs":

"No A.A. member should 'play doctor'; all medical advice and treatment should come from a qualified physician.

Appropriate use of medication for addiction treatment (MAT) can be lifesaving and should be prescribed for suitable individuals by an informed and qualified physician or other prescriber.

QUESTION 13: After I successfully complete treatment for a substance use disorder, how long must I stay sober before you determine I am totally cured?

ANSWER: At this time, there is no method to permanently "cure" an individual diagnosed with a substance use disorder. Permanent abstinence from mood-altering substances should be considered the long-term treatment of choice for this chronic, relapsing, and potentially fatal illness.

QUESTION 14: Do people with substance addiction still need counseling or monitoring after treatment? You are the medical director of the Ohio Professionals Health Program (OhioPHP). How long does your organization case manage, follow up, and monitor your assigned clients?

ANSWER: Generally, for most licensed healthcare professionals (and other safety-sensitive professions), monitoring for one to five years is recommended. Data has shown that, specifically for physicians, five years of therapeutic monitoring can improve the sustained recovery rate from about 50 percent in the first year to as high as 85–90 percent over five years.

QUESTION 15: What is your opinion and experience with substance addiction medicine such as naltrexone or Vivitrol®, methadone and Suboxone® (buprenorphine)? What do you recommend as measures to prevent the abuse of medically prescribed drugs?

ANSWER: When properly prescribed by a trained and experienced clinician, misuse or "abuse" of these medications is rare.

QUESTION 16: I have read a lot lately about some authors championing the value of "controlled drinking" methods to aid alcohol misuse. "Dry January" or "personal weekly drinking schedules" are a couple examples. Do you support controlled drinking efforts like these, or do you maintain abstinence as the best policy?

ANSWER: For those who are "only" misusing alcohol periodically, these may be somewhat beneficial in some circumstances. However, for those who truly have an alcohol use disorder, these methods provide no benefit whatsoever, except perhaps to demonstrate to the individual that "controlled drinking" is not possible for them.

DO OUR CURRENT POLICIES CONTRIBUTE TO RELAPSE?

Current public resource commitments toward the treatment of addiction are misdirected, inadequate, and often painfully wasted. Here is a summary of the absurdity of our present national approach.

- The vast majority of people with a substance use disorder relapse multiple times without any treatment. Of the small minority who are treated, their opportunities are generally short-term and medically inadequate in quality and overall effectiveness. High relapse rates are almost assured without any treatment or with insufficient treatment. Each relapse results in multiplying the personal and societal costs listed above along with the associated human suffering.
- The incidence rate of alcohol and drug use connected to the legal offenses for which people are arrested, jailed, imprisoned and/or institutionalized in the US is very high. Billions of dollars in societal costs spent for the crime and punishment treatment of people with a chronic, progressive disease is staggering; and unless effectively treated during their imprisonment (highly unlikely), these same people will often repeatedly relapse and become "repeat" offenders.
- The majority of individuals with an alcohol use disorder do not commit violent crimes. Yet, a number of the consequential incidents or accidents committed by people with alcohol abuse disorders occur most often when they are actively under the influence, in a state of painful withdrawal or experiencing a blackout.
- Overwhelmingly people in the US suffering substance addiction do not receive financial help for treatment.

Relapse is the product of misdirected public policy!

Unfortunately, with both untreated addiction rampant and unregulated care widespread in the United States, there are "experts" who see addiction treatment as an area ripe for quick profits. Using financial shortcuts, generating complications to qualify for payments or marketing appealing ideas like "cures" or "controlled" use, the extraordinarily low percentage of people who do seek help are subject to inadequate, low quality, and short-term care.

Many "rehabs" and general medical practices don't have sufficiently trained, qualified or experienced addiction doctors or other trained professional staff to deliver quality chronic care for the needed sufficient length of time. A considerable number of mainstream health professionals would rather not spend the necessary time required to identify, screen, or initially treat either alcoholics or addicts. These addiction disease-related tasks are difficult, time-consuming and don't usually qualify for adequate financial reimbursement in lieu of staff time spent. Ill-prepared and unmotivated for some legitimate reasons, too many of the current mainstream medical practice community systematically default in their screening responsibilities to first do no harm and second abdicate from providing chronic disease managed care.

The other extremely significant area in which our existing mainstream medical care is failing is with the prevention and care of individuals who have alcohol and prescription drug use disorders. These individuals are included in the group that I refer to as "silent sufferers." Scientific evidence has all the knowledge, tools and technology we need to significantly help these people. If only our mainstream medical community would commit to the following steps, our public health system could save millions of lives and billions of wasted dollars:

- A more welcoming and compassionate environment
- Increased outreach, earlier identification, and preliminary screening of new and existing patients
- Joint patient and family education
- Provision of screening and basic initial interventions
- Referrals to comprehensive assessments and quality, longer-term
- care and support
- Early integration of patient and family into disease education and
- area twelve-step or other community support groups
- Chronic disease managed care planning/monitoring in community collaborative care networks

The result of the difficulties dealing with addiction in mainstream medical practices has been the proliferation of an entirely separate, segregated, siloed, and largely unregulated health industry. The so-called "Wild West of Addiction Care" as a peripheral health enterprise has proliferated mainly outside of the usual institutional controls. Government oversight and any internal health industry oversight common to the norm of medical treatment and care for all other known chronic medical diseases is practically nonexistent.

Bottom line, our US medical establishment, including most of our colleges and medical schools, are failing to be directly involved in providing adequate training to treat the most prevalent, costly, and destructive chronic medical disease currently facing our nation.

Another major gap in addiction care within our present public health system is also apparent in its current referral and follow-up processes. Many doctors don't screen existing patients for substance use disorders. If a patient's symptoms somehow do become apparent, most medical practices that provide referral options don't adequately follow up to ensure proper chronic disease care management.

Think of this. The vast majority of our nation's health care doctors, practices, and professionals are, in daily practice, clinically disconnected from the growing national epidemic of addiction disorders. An increasing number of experts are sounding the alarm.

"The addiction crisis is even worse than the headlines convey," according to a May 31, 2024 article written by Caitlin Owens in *Axios*. The author substantiates this warning with facts that include the following:[66]

- The multidrug crisis of overdose deaths is centered on fentanyl often paired with other drugs, even animal tranquilizers. While over 100,000 overdose deaths are occurring every year from illegal drugs, which is double the number killed in the Vietnam War, alcohol regularly kills millions annually.
- Tens of millions misuse or are addicted to mind-altering substances and nearly 30 million have an alcohol use disorder. Over 17 percent of the twelve and over population have a substance use problem, and among young adults eighteen to twenty-five, that number jumps to 28 percent.

- An estimated 321,566 children have lost a parent to overdoses in the past decade, which in turn cause mass scarring from trauma and directly adverse economic impact, and obviously lost human potential.

The Hazelden Betty Ford Foundation, as recently as August of 2024, was reported by Laura Lovett, Editor of Behavioral Health Business, as "seeing an uptick" in the higher demand for withdrawal management and residential treatment services.[67]

In the August 19, 2024 issue of *Scientific American*, Allison Parshall reports that people are, often unintentionally, overdosing on semaglutide, a potentially lethal ingredient in the popular new weight loss drugs like Ozempic and Wegovy.[68]

Good news is surfacing in recent reports indicating that adolescent use of marijuana may be declining slightly. However, with every other age group, the indicators show both an increase in cannabis use and a corresponding increase in marijuana use disorder.

One more piece of relevant information published in *Alcohol Research: Current Reviews* finds that alcohol consumption, especially binge drinking, has been found "to initiate immune signaling and pro-inflammatory reactions in the brain that may contribute to disease development."[69]

These reports highlight our increasing societal problem with mind-altering substances, particularly legal ones. How much proof do we need to show the tremendous gap of what is actually occurring in our addictive reality and the absence of US mainstream medical practices, real quality disease treatment and adequate chronic care to stem the epidemic of legal substance use disorders.

Many treatment centers or clinics operate with inadequate staff, insufficient funding levels and fluctuating budgets to maintain the quality of care needed. Although the control of or cure for addiction has long been every alcoholic's or addict's delusional dream, it is so disappointing to realize that many "rehabs," many so-called "recovery centers," could be more aptly labeled "relapse factories" or short-term, addiction stimulators.

This would be comparable to a primary care practice either not screening at all for diabetes or eventually identifying a person with diabetes, referring that individual somewhere to an external, unregulated, unassociated clinic, and failing to ever monitor their blood sugar levels, their weight, or their dietary habits again. Somebody needs to follow up! All chronic disease patients need regular monitoring to increase the possibility of positive health change. Substance use disorder is no exception!

Some addiction "rehabs" allowed to operate today are downright criminal, bare-bones operations that rip off patients and insurance companies for days of minimal care, failing to provide integration with existing local twelve-step or other support programs, omit any family education, or don't provide patient follow-up and monitoring. In essence, many poor quality and short-term operations are tacitly increasing patient relapse and failure. And remember, every relapse leads to further disease progression, harmful consequences, and more financial waste.

In recent years there has been a growing movement among addiction care advocates to repair the immense failures of the outdated Nixon-era War-on-Drugs, that encouraged a "lock up all users" mentality. This movement is asking society—and especially its institutions—to treat people with substance disease as human beings, regardless of social status, income level, occupation, race, or culture, and even without regard to what their addictive substance is or its source.

MYTHS AND FACTS

Myths About Addiction

<u>Addiction is a "personality" disease</u>

Wrong! Addiction is a chronic, progressive, fatal (if untreated) physiological disease that attacks the brain, body, organs and central nervous system. Like other chronic disorders (such as diabetes, Parkinson's disease, or kidney disease), alcohol or drug addiction is not cured, only arrested. Even though it has psychological, social, environmental, mental, and spiritual aspects to be treated, substance use disorder has specific chemical, biological, and genetic causes. Treating it with only counseling is missing the core of the problem. No specific "personality" has been proven to be more susceptible to addiction.

<u>All it takes is a person to exhibit sufficient willpower to stop drinking or drug use.</u>

Wrong! Alcoholics and addicts have tremendous willpower, but it becomes obsessively misdirected toward obtaining the next drink or drug. Once the craving stage starts, and the "capture point" of hijacked brain systems occurs, willpower or conscious choice is no longer a factor in decision-making.

<u>Successful people don't often get addicted!</u>

Wrong! My "sponsor" or volunteer recovery coach is a highly successful professional. The guys I sponsor or "coach" include the CEO of a very large public health system, two highly successful insurance executives, a very well respected college basketball coach, a successful engineer, and other men who are having outwardly successful working or professional careers.

Oftentimes, "high functioning" or successful alcoholics/addicts are "too self-sufficient" and fail to seek help. But all successful folks who drink or use addictively eventually find success fleeting when "captured and imprisoned within the prison walls of addiction."

Dr. Whitney, who has treated thousands of addicted people, has told me that one of the most difficult subgroups of people he has dealt with are "the wealthy" because they have the resources to cover up their personal consequences. This, of course, prolongs their denial of a problem.

<u>It is okay for kids to experiment with alcohol at an early age, especially a drink given to them at home. This gets them accustomed to handling themselves and their liquor in a safe environment.</u>

Wrong! One of the primary risk factors that cause addiction is "the early age of onset," when a person drinks their first drink or uses their first addictive drug. The earlier one drinks or uses drugs, when the adolescent brain is underdeveloped, the higher the chance of acquiring a substance use disorder. Home or away, it is still an addictive substance.

<u>If you are genetically hardwired, have family history, there is little you can do to avoid addiction to alcohol or drugs.</u>

Wrong! Even if genetically predisposed, you don't have to suffer addiction. And you won't if you don't drink or use. Thirty percent of American adults do not drink at all.

<u>Once you quit drinking, relapse is almost inevitable, and necessary to eventually achieve sobriety. "Hitting rock bottom" is required before you seek help.</u>

Wrong! If you are having any problem stemming from alcohol or drug use, your elevator is already going down. But you can choose to stop the elevator and get off at any floor before you reach your basement, known as "the bottom." Many alcoholics are now seeking help before they experience every potential failure, pain, and loss the disease can eventually bring. And that is an endless list!

<u>As long as you limit consumption, control your drinking, or as alcohol ads suggest, "drink responsibly," you will avoid alcohol-related problems.</u>

Wrong! While brewery companies endorse this for obvious massive profit motives, the premise is false for 12 to 20 percent of drinkers who are alcoholics—and a higher percentage of those who are binge drinkers or problem drinkers, especially young people. Anyone in recovery will tell you that "one is too many and a dozen is not enough." Most of these drinkers have experienced some combination of tolerance, withdrawals, and a level of compulsion to drink. In other words, their brain is not totally functional when it comes to decision-making about drinking.

Many drinkers do not realize the actual effect alcohol has on them, including in areas of judgment, coordination, and inhibition. Numerous studies clearly show that a majority of drinkers underestimate the amount their cognitive skills are impaired. The result of this lack of accurate self-awareness is often trouble in the form of aggressiveness or violence, property damage, accidents (especially while driving), arguments, crime, and other irresponsible behavior.

<u>The kind of alcohol you drink has a lot to do with whether you develop an addiction to it. Wine is less likely to be addictive than beer and beer less likely than hard liquor.</u>

Wrong! Any alcohol is alcohol and is an addictive, mind-altering substance. Extensive use of any addictive drug (wine, beer, liquor, marijuana, cocaine, or heroin) causes substance use disorder to occur through the same stages: tolerance of the drug, withdrawal from the drug into negative effects, and an obsessive craving for the drug. To the brain, any alcoholic drink, regardless of kind, is ethanol.

Due to genetics, environment, and other factors, if you develop an addiction, you won't be drinking just a glass of wine, one bottle of beer, or a whiskey sour at one sitting.

Alcohol is a drug. Addictive drugs all cause physiological adaptations in the brain through the same developmental stages. In this regard, all alcohol and drugs have the potential to be addictive.

<u>When you stop drinking or using addictive drugs, the addiction goes away.</u>

Wrong! Once a person has consumed enough to have experienced the three developmental stages of addiction, the disease is physiologically entrenched and never fully disappears with abstinence. Never cured, only arrested!

The recovery community has many examples of its members not drinking for over twenty years, then unexplainably deciding to have a drink somewhere and ending up worse off than when they previously quit decades before.

<u>Once adults are age sixty-five or older, the risk of alcoholism manifesting itself decreases considerably.</u>

Wrong! Just the opposite! The risk of the elderly becoming active alcoholics is higher than the normal population. My father is a prime example. (Read Coach's Story, page XX.)

<u>The stomach can be "coated" with grease or milk to prevent the absorption of alcohol into the brain/bloodstream.</u>

Wrong! A stomach being coated to absorb more alcohol or prevent harmful side-effects is wishful thinking; it doesn't happen.

Coach's Favorite Myths

<u>If you quit drinking on your own after intensive use, you are sober.</u>

Not really. We call people "dry drunks" who have quit drinking but still display many of the behavioral characteristics of an active alcoholic like restlessness, irritability, resentment, discontent, anger, and/or isolation and loneliness. Real sobriety includes living life to the fullest and making personal changes necessary to find serenity, happiness, freedom, and joy in life.

<u>If you quit drinking but smoke a little pot, you are sober.</u>

No! Substituting one addictive chemical for another, like "a marijuana maintenance plan," does not remove your substance use disorder, it just alters your drug of choice. The same is true if you substitute hard liquor with beer or wine. Same difference! Same delusion! I know!

<u>Drinking alcohol is not nearly as dangerous as using cocaine or heroin.</u>

Again, not true. Dr. Grisel refers to alcohol as "the sledgehammer" drug for a reason. It pounds you over a longer period of time before, if untreated, it kills you. Alcohol and tobacco use causes more deaths annually in the US than all other addictive drugs combined. Ironically, this "killer" drug is legal, promoted, accepted, and easily accessible.

Facts: Financial Burden of Alcohol

Worldwide annual revenues from alcohol sales exceed $150 billion and increased significantly during the recent COVID pandemic years. Anheuser-Busch/InBev Brewery has annually spent over forty-one million dollars in lobbying costs and political contributions. This is the same company that urges Americans to drink more, but "responsibly" of course.

In 2016, alcohol killed twice as many Americans as the combined total of prescription drugs, opioids, and heroin overdose related deaths. In 2018, over 3.3 million deaths worldwide were alcohol related, over 100,000 in the US. Also in 2018, in the US, drunk drivers were involved in 147 million accidents, and 17 per day were casualties as a result of alcohol-related crashes.

Staggering costs back in the year 2018:

- 442 billion dollars was spent on health care, lost productivity, and criminal justice in costs related to alcohol and drugs
- 66 billion dollars were spent on healthcare, $578 million on economic loss and $674 million on societal harm from alcohol related expenses
- US federal and state governments spent over 15 billion and US insurers spent 5 billion in alcohol-related expenses

Sources: All data and facts listed above are from the following sources:

- "Global Status Report on Alcohol and Health, 2018," The World Health Organization.
- Maté, Dr. Gabor, *In the Realm of Hungry Ghosts*, North Atlantic Books, 2010.
- "Sobering Facts," The Centers for Disease Control and Prevention, 2018.
- "The Surgeon General's Report on Drugs, Alcohol, and Health," US Department of Health and Human Services, 2016.

Other Generally Accepted Facts About Alcohol Use

- 30% of adults do not drink at all
- 30% of adults who drink but have less than one drink daily
- 40% of all college students binge drink monthly
- 80% of the world's adult population drinks but only 10 to 23% become alcoholics or binge/problem drinkers
- 12% or more American adults are battling a combination of alcohol (14.5 million) and/or other drug misuse (8.1 million)
- 10% of American adults fully meet the substance use disorder criteria
- The top 10% of American drinkers average 74 drinks per week, over 10 per day
- 22 million Americans have alcohol/drug addictions, more common than cancer
- There has been a distinct shift upward in the way Americans drink alcohol in the last 50 years due highly to increased accessibility (e.g., supermarkets), expansive marketing efforts, and public event receptivity (sports, celebrations, etc.)
- In recent years, the worldwide drinking rates have skyrocketed in all age groups.
- The two leading killer drugs in the world are legal in the US—tobacco and alcohol. These two drugs do more harm than any other combination of addictive drugs. today's illicit fentanyl is 50 times more potent than morphine.

GAMETIME ADJUSTMENTS: THE CURRENT STATE OF SUBSTANCE USE DISORDER TREATMENT AND RECOVERY

- For adolescents, every year beyond 13 years old that they go without alcohol or drugs, their likelihood of eventually being addicted declines by 5%. And 90% of individuals with current alcohol and other substance use disorders started using before 18 years old, when the brain isn't fully developed. Only 11% of young people (12 to 17 years old) have been in any drug education/prevention program.
- Less than 8% of Americans suffering from substance use disorder obtain any help, and, without formal treatment, less than 10% of those who attend AA stay sober for a year.
- People who do not quit smoking tobacco after they quit still have an 80% or more chance of relapse.

"More, Broader, Kinder, Earlier, Faster, Better, Longer!"

THE OPPONENT:
A LOADED ROSTER

THE OPPONENT'S ROSTER

BASIC LINEUP OF ADDICTIVE DRUGS

- Alcohol (Legal)
- Nicotine/Tobacco (Legal)
- Marijuana and Cannabis Products (Legal)
- Illicit Drugs
  - Cocaine including "crack"
  - Opioids including heroin and fentanyl
  - Hallucinogens, including LSD, PCP, psilocybin, Ecstasy, mescaline, and peyote
  - Methamphetamines, including crystal meth
  - Hashish
  - Synthetic Drugs, including "bath salts," "K2," and "Spice"
- Prescription Type Drugs (Legal)
  - Pain Relievers, such as opioids fentanyl, codeine, oxycodone, hydrocodone, and tramadol
  - Tranquilizers, such as benzodiazepines (Valium, Xanax, Ativan, Lunesta) and muscle relaxers
  - Stimulants and methamphetamines
- Over the Counter and Other Harmful Drugs (Legal)
  - cold cough medicines, inhalants, gasoline, nitrous oxide, general anesthetics (ketamine), and solvents

THE OPPONENT ROSTER: ALCOHOL

Characteristics

- Sold: Legally
- Marketed: Intensely
- Class: Often labeled as a sedative/hypnotic and, at times, a stimulant

- Description: The best descriptive for alcohol is "a disinhibitor;" a stimulant/ sedative
- Administration: Orally

Initial Effect

- When the blood alcohol level is rising, a stimulant effect often occurs largely the result of disinhibition and produces a feeling of arousal or excitement
- When the blood alcohol level falls, arousal decreases and an antianxiety, subdued hypnotic state develops (therefore alcohol can speed you up and then slow you down)

Brain/body impact

- Low doses - disinhibition, reduced anxiety, relaxation
- Higher doses - sedation, sleep, passing out, blacking out, and brain cell damage
- Intoxication with impaired judgment, sense of pleasure, slurred speech, confusion, moodiness, imbalance, vomiting, hangover, alcohol respiration through skin, and/ or effects on cognition, emotional, memory, and movement systems

Physiology

- GABA receptors facilitate inhibition
- Norepinephrine production causes stimulation
- Water solubility of alcohol causes its distribution into all body organs and brain regions
- Beta-endorphins produce euphoria
- Glutamate (brain energy) activity is impeded, consequently harming new memory formation
- Neuroactivity throughout the brain/body slowed
- Excitatory electrical activity in neurons slowed
- Chemical communications and cell connections in the brain impeded
- Damage to the liver and heart from ethanol metabolism

RECENT RESEARCH: ALCOHOL

Unless otherwise specified, all dates listed are when findings were posted on Science Daily "Alcoholism News"

- "The More Recent the Last Drink, the More Severe the Brain Disruption, the More Likely the Alcoholic Will Resume Drinking."
  - The longer the abstinence, the more the brain interference in the decision-making region diminishes. This contradicts the concept of controlled drinking.

A 2020 study by LH. Rajih Sinha, Sarah K. Blaine (Auburn University, key author et. al.)

- "Why One Day at a Time Works (for recovery from alcoholism) as a Mantra for AA and 12 Step Programs".
  - With alcohol use disorder, associative disruptions between the ventromedial prefrontal cortex and the striatum, a brain network, are linked to decision-making. The more recent the last drink, the more likely the alcoholic will drink again. Controlled drinking is again delegitimized.

A study at Yale University, 8/27/2020

- "Vitamin B Deficiency a Key Factor in the Development of Alcohol-Related Deficiency"
  - Deposits of iron were found in the brain resulting from vitamin B deficiency caused by alcohol use.

A study at the Medical University of Vienna, 9/20/2020

- "Low-Level Alcohol Use During Pregnancy Can Adversely Influence a Child's Brain Development"
  - A study demonstrated that a couple of drinks in pregnancy can have significantly adverse brain development in children.

University of Sydney, 9/25/2020

- "A Potential Game-Changer To Reverse Alcohol Intoxication, Accelerated Elimination Via The Lungs"
  - Normally 90 percent of alcohol is cleared by the liver at a constant rate that cannot be increased. When a certain level of blood alcohol concentration is reached, cellular and organ damage, even death, can occur. Currently, other than dialysis, no other method exists to remove alcohol from the blood.
  - "The University Health Network has recruited the lungs. The harder the breathing, the more alcohol is eliminated from the body. They found that hyperventilation can eliminate alcohol three times faster than the liver. They have developed a simple device that allows a patient to hyperventilate the alcohol while returning to the body the correct amount of carbon dioxide to reestablish normal levels of blood chemicals."

Article in The Nature Research Journal from researchers led by Dr. Joseph Fisher University Health Network 11/12/2

- "Chronic Alcohol Use Reshapes the Brain's Immune Landscape During Anxiety and Addiction"
  - The amygdala, the brain region involved in emotion, behavior, and motivation is strongly implicated in alcohol abuse. Significant changes to anti-inflammatory mechanisms and cellular activity were found to drive alcohol addiction.
  - Chronic use of alcohol compromises immune cells (protein interleukin 10) which are prevalent in the brain. These IL-10 cells ensure the immune system doesn't respond too powerfully to

disease. They also appear to influence key behaviors associated with chronic alcohol use.
- Dr. Paust determined the precise immune cells that were affected by the change from prolonged exposure to alcohol, corresponding to increased levels of microglia and T regulator cells which produce IL-10 protein. This work substantiates that the immune system responds uniquely to chronic alcohol use.

Scripps Research Institute Department of Molecular Medicine, Dr. Mariso Roberto, Dr. Reesha Patel, plus the work of Dr. Silke Paust, Scientific Reports 11/16/2020

- "Drinking Blocks a Chemical That Promotes Attention"
  - Alcohol diminishes the release of norepinephrine in the brainstem nucleus intended to aid focus. Persons under the influence are off-balance when they walk, but surprisingly the researchers found calcium activation in the Bergmann glia is not critical for motor coordination. The findings did support the critical role of the cerebellum and non-motor function roles and that glial cells are not only supporting basic brain maintenance, but they can also be participating in cognitive function as well. These are disrupted by alcohol.
  - This finding has implications for a more widespread range of normal brain functions that are adversely impacted by alcohol in addition to its role in dampening the inherent "vigilance" system of the brain.

A paper from the Texas Health Science Center at UT Health San Antonio, Senior authors Dr. Martin Paulhert and Dr. Manzoor Bhat, 12/2/2020

- "Direct Link Between Increased Hazardous Alcohol Drinking and Life Stresses Triggered by The COVID Pandemic"
  - The odds of heavy alcohol use increased an extra 19 percent with each week of "lockdown" from the pandemic in 2020. With people who don't drink excessively, the odds of intake increased by 28 percent. Among binge drinkers the growth was a staggering 60 percent due to "the isolation factor."
  - One of five high-wage earners, already a risk factor for hazardous alcohol consumption, reported a 20 percent increase in drinking. One in three adults reported recent binge drinking and self-reporting binge drinkers reported increasing episodes. Unquestionably, during the period studied, increased alcohol consumption and harmful drinking were accompanying the pandemic.

- "20% Uptick in US Alcohol Sales During Covid"
  - While alcohol sales have increased by 20 percent and excessive home drinking by 27 percent, food service and bar sales have decreased significantly. Police report an increase from 10 to 27 percent in domestic violence calls, depending on locale.

A study at the University of Michigan, 6/24/2021.

- "Binge Drinking Increase"
  - While binge drinking among women has not grown in recent years, the overall rate of American adults who binge drink, the number of binging incidents, and the binge drinking of US older men (ages 65 plus) has increased significantly due to separation, divorce, being widowed, and retirement.

Journal of the American Geriatrics Society, 12/8/2021

- "Link Between Youth with High Alcohol Sensitivity and Earlier Alcohol Use Disorder (AUD)"
  - Adolescents who report a high sensitivity to the pleasure and rewarding effects of alcohol are much more likely to develop AUD over the next ten years.

University of Chicago Medical Center, 1/5/2021.

- "Driving Impairment from Alcohol Drinker Perceptions"
  - Findings revealed that half of all drivers underestimate their impairment from drinking.

Study at the University of Cambridge, 12/6/2021

- "The "Brake" in Our Brain for Binge-Drinking"
  - A brain circuit that works as a "brake" on binge drinking plays a major role in a stress response network. This "brake" is reduced in effectiveness by alcohol binge drinking. Interestingly, the brain circuit in females acts more strongly as a "brake" to bingeing than in males.
  - Weill Cornell Medicine finding first appeared on August 23, 2021, in Nature Communication

- "Neural Roots/Origins of Alcoholism Identified"
  - The area that regulates our response to danger, senses unpleasant or emergency situations, is the medial orbitofrontal cortex (mOFC) at the front of the brain. A person is at greater risk of developing alcohol use disorder (AUD) when the brain's information pathway is imbalanced by either:
    - (a) Alcohol inhibiting dorsal periaqueductal gray (dPAG) at the brain's core, which causes processing adverse situations inefficiently, so the brain is unable to respond to negative signals. This leads a person to feel the benefits of drinking alcohol but not recognize its harmful side effects. This alcohol-induced inhibition is a probable cause of compulsive drinking.
    - (b) Alcohol can influence an overexcited dPAG at the brain's core that makes the person feel unpleasant or present an adverse situation in which they feel the need to escape, resulting in the impulse to seek alcohol for relief.

Findings of a British-Chinese collaborative effort of the University of Warwick, Cambridge and Fudan University in Shanghai, published originally in the Journal of Science Advances and posted 2/8/2021

- "New Study Links Moderate Alcohol Use with Higher Cancer Risk"
  - Moderate alcohol use was directly linked to cases of:
    - Breast Cancer: 24 percent of cases
    - Colon Cancer: 20 percent of cases
    - Rectal Cancer: 15 percent of cases
    - Oral Cancer: 13 percent of cases
    - Liver Cancer: 13 percent of cases

A worldwide study by the Centre for Addiction and Mental Health, Lancet Oncology funded by the World Health Organization International Agency for Research on Cancer, led by Harriet Rumgayetal, 7/14/2021

- "Brain Regions Responsible for Intoxicating Effects of Alcohol"
  - The alcohol that is not broken down in the liver enters the brain. This study measured the distribution of the Acetaldehyde Dehydrogenase (ALDH2) enzyme in the cerebellum which controls balance and coordination.
  - The ALDH2 enzyme controls the conversion of ALD into acetate in the brain, this interacts with the brain messenger chemical GABA which acts to decrease activity in the nervous system. This decrease in activity results in drowsiness, impaired coordination, and reduced inhibitions.

University of Maryland School of Medicine, published in Nature Metabolism, April 14, 2021

- "Connection Between Addictive Drugs and Brain Function in Mice
  - Researchers from the University of Chicago and the US Department of Energy's Argonne National Laboratory discovered specific changes that occur in the brains of mice exposed to cocaine.
  - These insights into the function of dopamine neuron structures have advanced researchers' understanding of how certain types of addictions operate and have buoyed the possibilities of developing treatments for them.
  - This research is involved in the growing field of "connectomes" using highly advanced 3D maps of all neurons in the brain and their connections.
  - Findings of this research:
    - Verify the process by which dopamine is transmitted across neurons in extracellular space, not marking conventional physical connections where signals are transferred across synapses
    - Found dopamine neurons don't make physical connections as previously thought
    - Discovered with cocaine, the widespread anatomical changes from the response to drugs happen almost immediately and more pervasively. Summary: non-synaptic communication and axonal remodeling occur after cocaine exposure.

Medical Press, published in eLite Journal, written by John Spizzim, 1/18/22

- "More Alcohol, Less Brain (even with an average of just one drink daily)".
  - People who drink heavily have alterations in brain structure and size that are associated with cognitive impairment. In an analysis of data from a survey of more than 36,000 adults, even a few beers or glasses of wine per week carry risks to the brain. A team led by researchers from the University of Pennsylvania found that light-to-moderate alcohol consumption was associated with overall brain volume.

Published in Medical Press, Addiction News, 3-4-22; researchers include Gideon Nave, Reagan Wetherill, and Henry Kranzler of the University of Pennsylvania, Remi Daviet of the University of Wisconsin-Madison et. al.

- "Paternal Alcohol Used Increases Frequency of Fetal Development Issues"
  - This study found the epigenetic factor of prenatal exposure to alcohol in the male can manifest in the placenta, which supplies nutrients to the growing fetus. With paternal alcohol exposure, placentas become overgrown. Although the information is passed on to the fetus from the father, the mother's genetics and the sex of the offspring also play a role.

Published in the FASEB Journal, Nov. 2021, Dr. Michael Golding, Texas A&M College of Veterinary Medicine and Biomedical Sciences.

- "A Hormone Produced by the Liver Suppresses Alcohol Consumption in Monkeys"
  - A hormone, fibroblast growth factor 21 (FGF21), produced by the liver in monkeys that have a strong preference for alcohol, suppresses the alcohol consumption. The study also found that the protein known to also reduce sugar intake, acts on different brain circuits to reduce alcohol and sugar consumption in the amygdala (reward-seeking behavior) and the nucleus accumbens (reward and addiction).

Published in Cell Metabolism from work led by Matthew Pothaff and Kyle Flippo (Univ. of Iowa Carver College of Medicine) and Drs. Gillum and Trammell (Univ. of Copenhagen).

- "Spirituality Circuit in the Brain Has Been Identified"
  - Investigators found that "spiritual acceptance" can be localized in a brainstem region, periaqueductal gray (PAG) that has been implicated in fear conditioning, brain modulation, altruistic behaviors, and unconditional love. Dr. Ferguson suggested that "spirituality, and religiosity are rooted in fundamental new biological dynamics . . . deeply woven into our social fabric." The investigators "were astonished that the brain circuit for spirituality is centered in one of the most evolutionary preserved structures of the brain."

Dr. Michael Ferguson, Brigham and Women's Hospital, Neuroscience News

- "Beyond Dopamine: Neuro Reward Circuitry Discovered"
  - In this study, researchers found that approximately 30 percent of the cells in the ventral teg-

mental area (VTA) are GABA neurons. This supports the idea that "there is another pathway than dopamine that likely plays a key role in rewards and reinforcements"; thus, "VTA GABA neurons involved in rewards and aversion can be potential targets for the treatment of addiction, depression and other stress-linked disorders."

Dr. Michael Bruchas, Univ. of Washington School of Medicine, paper in Nature Neuroscience, 2021

- "Using Alcohol and Marijuana Together Exacerbates Negative Consequences in Young Adults"
  - A study at Brown University and Rutgers University compared the negative consequences of college students who engaged in simultaneous alcohol and marijuana use and those who used only alcohol. Their primary findings were:
    - College students who used alcohol and marijuana simultaneously experience more negative consequences than those who use both substances sequentially.
    - Young adults drank more alcohol on days when they also used marijuana than on days when they only drank alcohol.

William Ross Perlman, Ph.D., National Inst. on Drug Abuse

- "Alcohol Use Among Women"
  - Recent studies of alcohol use among women have concluded that:
    - A woman is more likely to harm her health with long-term drinking than a man.
    - Women who drink heavily are more at risk than men for alcohol-induced injuries and accidental deaths.
    - Women progress more quickly along the spectrum of substance use disorder than men.
    - Women who drink heavily are more likely to become victims of violence and sexual assault.
    - The rates of binge and heavy drinking for women have increased over the last several years, especially for older adults.

Butler Center for Research, Hazelden Betty Ford Foundation December, 2017

Alcohol Use in 2023

In the survey, "binge drinking" was considered to be five or more drinks for men or four or more drinks for women in a single occasion. Binge drinking for five or more days by men or women is considered "heavy drinking."

In 2023, 134.7 million (47.5 % of people, aged twelve or older) reported they drank alcohol in the past month. Nearly half of these individuals were binge drinkers at least once in the past month. And, 16.4 million (12.2 percent) were heavy drinkers. Over one in four binge drinkers (26.7 percent) are heavy drinkers.

Regarding race and ethnicity factors, the percentage of white people is higher in using tobacco products, vaped nicotine, and heavy drinking, while there was little separation among races in the percentages of binge drinking. The use of most substances was lowest among Asians.

- **Underage Use of Alcohol** for Ages 12 to 20 in the Past Month
    - 5.6 million young people (15%) drank alcohol
    - 3.3 million young people (9%) binge drank
    - 663 thousand young people (1.7%) were heavy drinking
    - White youth had the highest incidence of drinking alcohol
- **Underage Use of Marijuana**
    - 15.4% of youth (ages 12 to 20) used marijuana
    - 25% ages 18 to 25 used marijuana
    - 5.6% of youth vaped marijuana, which is 1 in 3 young marijuana users

All data in this section is from the 2023 US Survey on Drug Use and Health, SAMHSA

OTHER BASIC TYPES OF DRUGS

Key Substance Use Indicators in The United States for 2023

Among people twelve or older in 2023, in excess of 167 million people, nearly 60 percent, used a mind-altering substance, including alcohol, nicotine, marijuana, and illicit drugs.

- **Legal Drug Use** In the Last Month
    - 134.7 million people or 48% of adults, 12 and over, drank alcohol
    - 49.9 million people or 18% used tobacco products
    - 26.6 million people or nearly 10% vaped nicotine
    - **Marijuana Use**
    - 43.6 million people in the past month
    - 61.8 million people in the past year
- **Illegal Drug Use**
    - Hallucinogens   8.8 million people
    - Cocaine   1.8 million people
    - Methamphetamines   1.6 million people
    - Heroin   0.4 million people
    - Fentanyl   0.3 million people
- **Prescription Drug Misuse**
    - Pain Relievers   2.2 million people
    - Tranquilizer/ Sedative 1.2 million people

- Stimulant   1.2 million people

The numbers from this recent year are clear. The incidence of legal substance use, whether marijuana use is considered so or not, is far greater than illegal or misused prescription drug use.

The Opponent Roster: Sedatives / Hypnotics

- Slows down the function of the central nervous system
- A substance that induces sedation by reducing irritability or excitement and suppresses the central nervous system while slowing brain activity —Wikipedia
- The majority of sedatives increase GABA (inhibitory neurotransmitter) activity producing calm/relaxation or inducing sleep

Types of Sedatives	Examples of Drugs in class
Barbiturates	Phenobarbital
Benzodiazepines	Valium, Ativan, Xanax, Lunesta
Hypnotics	zolpidem
Antihistamines	hydroxyzine
General anesthetics	ketamine, Nitrous oxide
Herbal sedatives	cannabis
Methaqualone	cloroqualone
Muscle relaxants	baclofen, clonidine, gabapentin
Opiates and synthetic opioids (See below for more info)	codeine, fentanyl, hydrocodone, methadone, morphine, opium, oxycodone, tramadol
Antidepressants	nortriptyline, trazodone,
Antipsychotics	clozapine
Neurosteroids	ganaxalone, hydroxydione
Others	Bromide salts

- Risks of Sedative use
    - Sedative dependence/use disorder
    - Drug misuse including drug overdose and combined drug intoxication
    - Dangers of combining sedatives and alcohol
    - Worsening of psychiatric symptoms
    - Dementia
    - Amnesia

- Disinhibition and crime

The Opponent Roster: Opiates

Opiates:

- Definition: a special class of drugs (known as painkillers or narcotics) naturally found in the opium poppy plant; effects found in both prescription meds and "street drugs" like heroin and fentanyl
- Effects of Opiate Use
  - Pain relief
  - Relaxation
  - Happy or high feelings
  - Constipation
  - Slowed breathing
  - Confusion
  - Nausea
  - Craving
  - Drowsiness
  - Overdose

Most common opioids

Prescription drugs:	Vicodin, morphine, OxyContin, hydrocodone, oxycodone, Buprophre, codeine, methadone, tramadol
Fentanyl	Often sold as an off-brown colored powder, 80 to 100 times more potent than morphine; mixed with cocaine, methamphetamines, animal tranquilizers, and other chemicals
Heroin	An illegal opiate drug made from poppy plants
	Sold as a white or brown powder or a black sticky substance known as "black tar" heroin. Can be injected, snorted, sniffed, or smoked. Often mixed with additives such as starch, sugar, or powdered milk; mixed with cocaine for "speedballing."
	Enters the brain rapidly with a "rush of euphoria" and binds to receptors and other cells in brain and body involved with the pleasure/pain system and controls heart rate, sleeping, and breathing.

Effects of Opioid Use

Short-Term	<ul><li>Dry mouth</li><li>Nausea and vomiting</li><li>Warm flushing of skin</li><li>Heaving feeling in arms/legs</li><li>Severe itching</li><li>Mentally clouded</li><li>Overdose</li><li>"Nodding" in and out of consciousness</li></ul>
Long Term	<ul><li>Restlessness</li><li>Infection of heart lining/valves</li><li>Insomnia</li><li>Severe muscle/bone pain</li><li>Collapsed veins</li><li>Male sexual dysfunction</li><li>Skin Abscesses</li><li>Female menstrual irregularity</li><li>Constipation</li><li>Severe cravings</li><li>Stomach cramps</li><li>Uncontrollable leg movements</li><li>Lung complications</li><li>Liver and kidney damage</li><li>Mental disorders such as depression and antisocial behavior</li></ul>

Fact: 4.6 percent of people who misuse prescription opioids switch to using heroin.

Sources for this section: Johns Hopkins Medicine, NIH, Rheanna Platt. Institute On Drug Abuse

The Opponent Roster: Stimulants

Stimulants:
- Definition: a substance that raises levels of physiological or nervous activity by speeding up the central nervous system (messages between the brain and body)
- Action: stimulants make a person feel more awake, alert, confident, or energetic by raising excitatory chemicals in the brain
- Forms: powder, tablet, crystals, capsules, liquid, intravenous injections
- Types of Stimulants:
  - Prescribed drugs in this class are used to treat ADHD, Diseases like Narcolepsy, et al
  - some are used for performance-enhancing drugs (PEDs) and Sfocus assistance.

THE OPPONENT: A LOADED ROSTER

Amphetamines and Methamphetamines
- Extremely addictive
- Usually smoked or ingested
- Commonly used in the past for depression, narcolepsy, and obesity
- Examples: speed, crystal meth (ice), Uppers, PEDs
- Illegally produced as a mix of drugs, binding agents, caffeine, and sugar

The Opponent Roster: Caffeine

- Definition: A natural chemical found in coffee, tea, chocolate, cocoa, candy, energy drinks
- Is physically addictive
- Works by stimulating the central nervous system, heart, muscles, and blood pressure; also can act as a diuretic (water pill)
- Effectively used for migraines, tension, and post-op headaches, pauses in breathing, low heart rates of newborns, mental alertness
- Possibly effectively used for athletic performance, diabetes, and infant lung disease, diabetes, memory, obesity, acute pain
- Side effects include insomnia, nervousness, restlessness, nausea, increased heart rate, headache, anxiety, chest pain, fatigue, irritability

The Opponent Roster: Cocaine

- Definition: an illegal psychoactive drug made from the leaves of coca trees and is powerfully addictive
- Rapidly absorbed by being snorted, inhaled, injected, or taken orally; reaches the brain quickly and is distributed to other tissues in the body
- Cocaine is rapidly metabolized by enzymes in the liver plasma in 30 to 60 minutes
- Also known as coke, blow, crack
- As a street drug, cocaine looks like a fine white crystal powder; it is often mixed with cornstarch, talcum powder, or flour to increase profits or it is combined with amphetamine or synthetic opioids like fentanyl
- Ways to use cocaine
    - People often use cocaine by snorting through the nose, rubbing it into their gums, or injecting it, sometimes combined with heroin (aka speedball); "freebase cocaine" is also a popular method to smoke cocaine that has been processed into rock crystals
- How cocaine affects the brain
    - The drug increases levels of the natural chemical messenger "dopamine" in brain circuits related to the control of movement and reward

Effects of Cocaine

Short-term Behavioral Effects	<ul><li>Extreme happiness and energy</li><li>Mental alertness</li><li>Hypersensitivity to sight, sound, touch</li><li>Irritability</li><li>Distrust of others, paranoia</li><li>Overdose</li></ul>
Health Effects	<ul><li>Restlessness</li><li>Infection of heart lining/valves</li><li>Insomnia</li><li>Severe muscle/bone pain</li><li>Collapsed veins</li><li>Male sexual dysfunction</li><li>Skin Abscesses</li><li>Female menstrual irregularity</li><li>Constipation</li><li>Severe cravings</li><li>Stomach cramps</li><li>Uncontrollable leg movements</li><li>Lung complications</li><li>Liver and kidney damage</li><li>Mental disorders such as depression and antisocial behavior</li></ul>
Long-term Effects	<ul><li>Loss of smell, nosebleeds, runny nose, and difficulty swallowing</li><li>Cough, asthma, respiratory problems</li><li>Severe bowel decay</li><li>Higher risk of HIV, Hepatitis C (via IV use)</li><li>Skin infections (IV use)</li><li>Scarring or collapsed veins (IV use)</li></ul>
Withdrawal symptoms	<ul><li>Depression</li><li>Fatigue</li><li>Increased appetite</li><li>Unpleasant dreams</li><li>Insomnia</li><li>Slowed thinking</li></ul>

The Opponent Roster: Nicotine

- Definition: A legal stimulant drug that speeds messages between the brain and the body, it is the main psychoactive ingredient in tobacco
- Side products from burning tobacco
    - Tar
    - Carbon Monoxide (CO), a toxic gas
    - Common Tobacco products with nicotine
    - Cigarettes
    - Cigars
    - Pipe tobacco
    - Chewing tobacco and nicotine pouches
    - Wet and dry snuff
    - Electronic cigarettes

Side Effects Of Nicotine

Short-term	<ul><li>Mild stimulation</li><li>Increased concentration</li><li>Increase in heart rate</li><li>Relaxation</li><li>Coughing</li><li>Dizziness</li><li>Bad breath</li><li>Headaches</li><li>Reduced appetite</li><li>Tingling and numbness in toes and fingers</li><li>Stomach cramps</li><li>Vomiting</li></ul>
Long-term	<ul><li>Cancers</li><li>Blindness/cataracts</li><li>Stroke</li><li>Birth defects</li><li>Periodontitis</li><li>Aortic aneurism</li><li>Pneumonia</li><li>Coronary heart disease</li><li>Diabetes</li><li>Respiratory diseases</li><li>Reduced fertility</li><li>Hip fractures</li><li>Male sexual dysfunction</li><li>Rheumatoid arthritis</li><li>Immune diseases</li><li>Addiction</li></ul>
Withdrawal Symptoms of Nicotine	<ul><li>Cravings</li><li>Anxiety</li><li>Irritability</li><li>Depression</li><li>Sleep problems</li><li>Increased eating</li><li>Poor concentration</li><li>Headaches</li><li>Coughing</li><li>Sore throat</li><li>Aches/pains</li><li>Upset stomach/bowel problems</li></ul>

Nicotine Notes: There are 59 million smokers in the US today. 500,000 annually have smoking-related illnesses. There are 700 chemicals in a cigarette, of which 200 are identified as toxic. 15.3 percent of all US male adults, 12.7 percent of females, smoke, and over 20 percent of high school students vape.

The bad news is 1.63 million school-age kids are smoking e-cigarettes each month. The good news is this is a reduction of over 20 percent usage than a year ago. But the worse news is the number of everyday vapers among children is increasing along with the number of kids using nicotine pouches.

The public marketing to attract these children at an early age is fierce. Unfortunately athletes and other public figures are being paid to promote oral nicotine pouches for kids. Although these pouches may have no tobacco in them, they are not without risk.

I chewed tobacco beginning at age 16 and smoked cigarettes at age 14, and then later cigars. I can testify firsthand of the dangers of these products, not only with my heart and lung issues, but with the fact that I was treated for problematic "spots" on the inside of my left cheek.

It seemed back then that chew and lip snuff would be relatively harmless compared to smoking tobacco. But, if you really want to know the truth without illusion, go visit a cancer hospital where mouth, lip, face, and throat cancers are treated, and look at the patients lined up in the waiting rooms. It is a scary awakening to what nicotine in any form can do to your face and neck. Although I stopped all forms of tobacco use many years ago, I am currently being monitored by specialists for mouth cancer due to the appearance of white spots on the inside of my cheeks.

The Opponent Roster: Psychoactive Drugs

Hallucinogens/Psychedelics

- Definition: a psychoactive agent that causes hallucinations, perceptual anomalies, and other substantial, subjective changes in thought, emotion, and consciousness that are not typically experienced to such degrees as other drug classes
- Classic psychedelic states cause increased empathy, visual distortions, ego dissolution, and mystical or spiritual experiences.
- Hallucinogens affect your senses and change the way you hear, see, taste, smell, and feel things.
- Traditional hallucinogens include LSD, psilocybin, and mescaline. All are derived from natural products: LSD from a fungus that often contaminates wheat and rye flavor; psilocybin comes from several types of mushrooms; and mescaline occurs naturally in certain cacti plants. Most hallucinogens, with a few exceptions, are illegal.
- Common Side Effects
    - LSD – Hallucinations, anxiety/depression, flashbacks, rapid heart rate/increased body temperature, dilated pupils, high blood pressure, extreme mood changes, overdose, psychosis, nausea, lack of appetite, sleep loss, tremors, and seizures
    - Psilocybin – Hallucinations, panic attacks, psychosis, nausea/vomiting, muscle weakness, lack of coordination, overdose

Marijuana/Cannabis Products

- Definition: a psychoactive drug from the dried flowers, leaves, stems, and seeds of the cannabis plant native to central and south Asia but now grown domestically in natural and synthetic environments. Of the more than 500 chemicals in marijuana, THC is responsible for the mind-altering effects of the drug; it is this THC chemical that creates distortions of the mental perceptions of the world and makes a person "high." Most often it is smoked, eaten, or vaporized.
- Other names include weed, pot, dope, hash, gummies
- Facts about marijuana
    - Since the early nineties the average THC content in marijuana has quadrupled in potency.
    - Extracts and resins from the marijuana plant have three to five times more THC than in the plant itself.
    - When smoked or vaporized THC passes quickly from the lungs to the bloodstream and throughout the body including the brain. Effects are felt almost immediately and can last from 1 to 3 hours. When eaten or drank, effects appear 30 to 60 minutes later.
    - The effects of edibles last much longer than smoking.
    - THC works on the communication network in the brain which is important for normal brain development and function (the endocannabinoid system).
    - In Ohio, prior to official adult legalization sales, there was, in the first six months of 2024, a nearly 50 percent increase in children under age six being exposed to edibles; also law enforcement officials are reporting a significant increase in driving under the influence due to marijuana product use
    - Addiction rate of marijuana users is approximately 10 percent
- Uses of medical marijuana treatment
    - THC: nausea and vomiting from chemotherapy
    - CBD (oil): seizures in children with epilepsy
    - THC and CBD: a mouth spray available in several countries outside the USA to treat symptoms and pain of multiple sclerosis
    - Chronic pain relief

Effects Of Marijuana

Initial Effects	• The "high" • Lack of coordination • Disrupted learning • Changes in perception/mood • Difficulty thinking
Short-Term Psychological Effects	• Altered senses of color and time • Increased appetite • Trouble thinking, solving problems • Delusions • Mood changes • Slow reactions • Memory problems • Loss of balance and coordination • Hallucinations • Psychosis
Long Term Effects	• Increased heart rate • Increased risk of mental health problems • Lack of appetite/weight loss • Reduced performance • Use of other drugs • Severe nausea and vomiting • Irritability • Sleeplessness • Respiratory problems • Lower birth weights and increased risk of behavioral problems in babies • Relapse • Reduced life satisfactions • Impaired driving • Mild withdrawal • Anxiety • Drug cravings

MDMA (Molly or Ecstasy)
- Definition: a synthetic drug that alters mood and perception; is chemically similar to both stimulants and hallucinogens and produces feelings of increased energy, pleasure, emotional warmth, and distorted sensory and time perception
- Ways of Use: capsule or tablet, liquid form, or powder snorted; often taken in combination with alcohol or marijuana
- In the brain, MDMA increases the activity of:
  - Dopamine: increased energy, reinforced behaviors in the reward system
  - Norepinephrine: increases heart rate, blood pressure
  - Serotonin: affects mood, appetite, sleep, sexual arousal, increased trust, emotional closeness and empathy, elevated mood
- Other side effects of Ecstasy include:
  - Nausea
  - Muscle cramping
  - Blurred vision
  - Involuntary teeth-clenching
  - Chills
  - Sweating
- Over the course of a week of MDMA use, a person can experience:
  - Irritability
  - Anxiety
  - Impulsiveness
  - Memory and attention problems
  - Aggression
  - Decreased appetite
  - Sleep problems
  - Decreased interest in and pleasure from sex
  - Spike in body temperatures
  - Liver, kidney or heart failure
  - Unsafe sexology

"More, Broader, Kinder, Earlier, Faster, Better, Longer!"

POSTGAME ANALYSIS:
APPENDICES AND REFERENCES

ACKNOWLEDGMENTS

My gratitude for a loving, safe and well-parented childhood home - my father, my mother, my brother, my grandparents, aunts, uncles, cousins, teachers and coaches for a foundation that has greatly enriched my life

For their enduring love and support, my wife Beverly; my wonderful children and their spouses, Matt and Kathy Wince, Susannah Wince and Amanda and Colin Baker; and my terrific grandchildren Olivia Peterson, (Luke), Elijah Wince, Isaiah Wince, Evelyn Wince, Emma Lee, Abigail Lee, Xavierie Baker, Liam Baker and Bodhi Baker

Special thanks to my grandkids Olivia, Elijah, Abigail and Evelyn for their typing, graphics, general tech support and patience with me.

Special thanks also to the following:

I am extremely grateful to Greg Cowles, our structural and language editor who has been a Godsend to me and our work at Champions. He has spent countless hours dedicated to arranging and completing this book in order to carry the recovery message of hope to others.

The Westerville Ohio Public Library staff of Erik, Elizabeth, Kristin, Mindy, Jessica, Adrian, Debbie, Dave, Catie and others

The past and present staff at Licking Memorial Health Systems, Shepherd Hill Campus and their life-saving help for our family beginning with great counselors Ellen Labas and Steve Gifford, former family program coordinators Ellen Miller and Dr. Wendy Flowers, all of the aides, the past and current administrative leaders including Tom Brennon, Erik Hockenberry and Rochelle Spangler, the secretaries in cottage A and B, and the outstanding addiction medicine doctors that have practiced there, ranging from founder Dr. William Kennedy to Drs. John Stang, Fred Karaffa, Richard Whitney and presently Dr. Andy Highberger with the support of LMHS Vice Presidents Dr. Craig Cairns, Benjamin Broyles and Greg Wallis

My great friend, Donald D. Hill and his terrific family, as well as Dr. Thomas Petryk, Dr. William McFarren, Dr. Mukesh Shah, Dr. Robert Raker, and two former players, now wonderful doctors, Kevin Graham and Dan Jonas

Three special men who mentored me for many years, Robert Schenk, Ben Rader and Richard Whitney.

My partners in the Champions Substance Recovery System organization: Andrew Anderson, Josh Shaffer and Greg Cowles

The old-timers who welcomed me and nurtured me through the early and very difficult days of my recovery- Amos P., Dave Wa., Roger, Sue, Ben, Pat , J.C.B., Barry., Karen, Jim W., Anne K., Johnny W. and others

Men who have trusted and inspired me in recovery-Andrew A., Bill W., B.J.D., Rick N., Mike C., Joe W., Brian D.,Josh S., Bill K., Mitch S.,Tyler A., Chas C. et. al.

All the members of the 12 step community groups in Newark, Granville, Heath, Johnstown, Worthington and Westerville for being there for me on a regular basis

Reverends Bruce Henderson, Charlie Daugherty, Gary Stratman, Karen Chakoian, Mrs. Carol Weiss and Dick Ellsworth, as well as Dr. Vergil Lattimore and Paul Chilcote formerly of the Methodist Theological Seminary of Ohio for their guidance and ministry; and the Joe Wojik, Johnny Carlisle and other families

The wonderful Central Ohio Rural Consortium (CORC) staff, and the dedicated board members whose work proudly benefited the east- central Ohio area for nearly a quarter of a century

The great young men I have been so privileged to coach in junior high, high school and college, and some terrific assistant coaches, trainers and friends over the years- Jim Cooper, Don Dolwick, Jim Dumbauld, Jeff Mills, Dave Parkhill, Scott Smith, Don Thorp, and others

Bev's longtime "Soul Sisters", Wendy Flowers and Jenny Richards

A special group known as the "The Fat Guys", my long-time brothers from around the country who continue to support me and my work—Larry Brown, David Fox, Chuck Seagle, Bob McCarthy, Bret Halverson, Bob Kerr, William Schmieder, Jeff Bridges, Mike Carr, Bill Wilkins, Steve Trippe, Mike Simmons, Jerry McCabe and Pete Cameron

Our special neighbors who have supported Bev and I -the Stare family, the Boffas, Gabrielle Vonville and Kevin Minner, Dave and Cinda Widder, Don and Barb Delwick

Many thanks to my copy editor Jennifer Pellman

Emily Hitchcock and Clair Fink of the Columbus Publishing Company, the kindest, most patient and encouraging publishers a rookie author could have, and Larry Buttermore for encouraging me to publish

Last but not least, my champions...former Lincoln Junior High running back/linebacker, a lifelong friend, Donald Eric Lee, and former basketball power forward ,Charles Claggett III, unquestionably my heroes and inspirations

To my Higher Power and all of you who have made such a positive difference in my life. Thanks and prayers.

ABOUT THE (COACH) AUTHOR

Gregory D. Wince

After graduating with honors from high school in Newark, Ohio, Greg Wince attended Bowling Green State University where he was a walk-on member of the freshman basketball squad. He transferred to Otterbein University where he played football and baseball, graduating with a BS in Education. It was there where he met his wife of fifty-six years, Beverly. They have three beautiful children and nine precious grandchildren.

Greg accepted a junior high school teaching position and coached three sports in his hometown. He obtained an MS in Education from Ohio University with a special interest in the emerging field of Black Studies, so he could better relate to the young people he was teaching and coaching.

Hired by Denison University as a part-time assistant coach, Greg recruited the first Black basketball players to the private Granville, Ohio college. During this period, Greg wrote his master's thesis on "The Social, Academic and Cultural Problems of the Black-Student Athlete in the Ohio Intercollegiate Athletic Conference."

Then Greg initiated a computer-assisted dropout prevention program for high-risk youth at Newark High School and subsequently embarked on two simultaneous careers that spanned the next twenty-three years.

His career in executive leadership began when he started a human resources organization. Central Ohio Rural Consortium Job Training (CORC), which provided employment, skills training/retraining, and career opportunities for youth and adults in six east-central Ohio counties. The organization grew to have several thousand clients, hundreds of business accounts, a staff of over one hundred and a 12-million-dollar annual budget.

Later in his career, Greg had a special opportunity to study innovative Total Quality Management (TQM) through the Edwards Deming Institute, named for the legendary US statistician who helped transform the struggling Japanese auto industry into a world powerhouse.

The CORC organization received numerous local, state, and national awards. These included a Presidential Award from Ronald Reagan, the Outstanding US Youth Training Program award from the National Youth Professionals Institute, numerous US Department of Labor and Ohio Governor Awards, and several local Chamber of Commerce Pride Builder designations.

Greg was involved at the state and national policy levels. He was elected by his peers as the three-time chair of The Ohio State Workforce Directors, the Chair of the six-state Great Lakes Region Employment and Training Association, and as an Ohio representative to the US Department of Labor Advisory Council for fifteen consecutive years. As a member of several Ohio Governor's Workforce Councils, Greg testified on four occasions before US Senate and Congressional hearings regarding national workforce policy and legislation.

A guest seminar presenter, trainer, and panelist throughout the eastern United States, his later consulting work focused upon organizational training and development.

Greg's second and parallel career was coaching men's college and high school basketball teams. His overall head coaching record was 294 wins and 65 losses. His teams won various championships and earned for him eight coach-of-the-year recognitions, including the AP Ohio High School Basketball Coach of the Year and several Ohio Central District coaching honors. His proudest accomplishment is the lifelong relationships with many of his former players and coaches.

Following retirement, Greg consulted with corporations and small businesses. On several occasions he accepted interim employment stints as the director youth programs at a local Presbyterian church, the executive director of a local mental health agency, and as a leader of a day center for developmentally disabled adults.

Greg returned to basketball as an assistant coach at Groveport- Madison High School and Ohio Dominican University, while attending the Methodist Theological Seminary of Ohio, where he concentrated on addiction ministry.

His new passion in later life has included learning about substance addiction, especially the crucial role of physiology in the disease and best practices for treatment and recovery.

For several years Greg led "Coach's Corner" educational discussions for patients in treatment settings. These sessions focused on the role of the brain in substance addiction, relearning through brain rewiring, behavioral change in recovery, and the role of spirituality in restoring positive relationships and life connections. He remains a public activist for improving substance addiction care. Greg is the founder of a new Champions Substance Recovery Systems, whose transformative purpose is to improve the identification, accessibility, availability, medical mainstreaming for longer term and better quality chronic medical disease care of individuals and families with alcohol and other substance use disorders.

"More, Broader, Kinder, Earlier, Faster, Better, Longer!"

ABOUT THE TEAM DOC

Richard N. Whitney, MD, DABAM, FASAM

Richard N. Whitney, MD, DABAM, FASAM, now serves as the medical director of the Ohio Professionals Health Program. This organization provides comprehensive assessment and referral services, as well as monitoring and advocacy, for licensed healthcare professionals throughout Ohio who have been diagnosed with addictive disorders or other impairing mental, emotional, behavioral, and/or physical illnesses.

Previously, Dr. Whitney practiced addiction medicine at Shepherd Hill, the behavioral health department of Licking Memorial Hospital in Newark, Ohio where he served as the Medical Director of Addiction Services there from 2001 until 2018. He is a frequent course instructor for the American Society of Addiction Medicine as well as a lecturer for a variety of professional and community organizations throughout the United States.

Dr. Whitney graduated from the University of Texas Southwestern Medical School in Dallas, Texas. He completed an internship in internal medicine at the University of Missouri-Kansas City School of Medicine in Kansas City, MO, followed by a residency in emergency medicine at Truman Medical Center, also in Kansas City.

Following his practice in emergency medicine, Dr. Whitney completed a fellowship in addiction medicine at Charter Hospital of Dallas in 1991 and has practiced addiction medicine since that time. He is a Diplomate of the American Board of Addiction Medicine and is a Fellow of the American Society of Addiction Medicine.

Dr. Whitney is married to Carol S. Whitney, PhD, an author and educator who specializes in the enrichment of gifted and twice-exceptional children and young adults. Dr. Whitney has three daughters and three grandchildren.

COMING SOON

COACH'S HANDBOOK VOLUME II:
"RECOVERY, A PRACTICAL SPIRITUALITY, AND A VISION OF HOPE"

- Essential strategies and skills to achieve a quality of recovery for the long term
- An individual path to a spiritual connection and reestablishing healthy relationships
- A transformational blueprint for government, health systems, health insurers, and our communities to provide more effective substance use disorder prevention and care

Link to this website csrsystems.org for the publication release date and to contact the staff of Champions Substance Recovery Systems with questions, suggestions and assistance.

RECOMMENDED READS ABOUT SUBSTANCE USE DISORDERS

ARTICLES

"2023 National Survey on Drug Use and Health Data Available." SAMHSA, US Dept. of Health and Human Services. July, 2024.

Barton, Antigone. 2023. "Florida Shuffle." Palm Beach Post, USA Today October 6.

"Facing Addiction in America: The Surgeon General's Report on Alcohol, Drugs and Health." SAMHSA, US Department of Health and Human Services, 2016.

Hargreaves et al. 2017. "Implementing SBIRT (Screening, Brief Intervention and Referral to Treatment)." *Public Health Reviews*, Open Access, BioMed Central.

Interlandi, Jensen and Damon Winter. 2023. "Help and Hope for People with Addiction." *New York Times*, December 17.

Owens, Caitlin. 2024. "The Addiction Crisis is Even Worse Than the Headlines Convey." *Axios*, May 31.

BOOKS

Grisel, Judith. *Never Enough: The Neuroscience and Experience of Addiction*. Doubleday Books, 2019.

Maté, Gabor. *In the Realm of Hungry Ghosts: Close Encounters with Addiction*. North Atlantic Books, 2020.

George F. Koob et al. *Drugs, Addiction, and the Brain*, Elsevier, 2014.

Kessler, David A., MD. *Capture: Unraveling the Mystery of Mental Suffering*. Harper Perennial, 2016.

The Addiction Spectrum, Paul Thomas, M.D. and Jennifer Marquis, M.D., Harper Collins, 2018

Dopamine Nation: Finding Balance in the Age of Indulgence, Dr. Anna Lembke, Penguin Random House, 2021

Undoing Drugs: How Harm Reduction is Changing the Future of Drugs and Addiction, Maia Szalavitz, Hatchette Books, 2021

Addiction Medicine, American Society of Addiction Medicine (ASAM), Oxford University Press,

Healing The Addicted Brain, Harold C. Urschel III, M.D. Sourcebooks Inc., 2009

<u>Understanding Science</u>: <u>Know Science</u>, <u>No Stigma</u>, Drs. Chuck Smith and Jason Hunt, Visualize Publishing, 2021

<u>The Power of Habit</u>, Charles Duhigg, Random House Trade Paperbacks, 2014

BEST PRACTICES OF SBIRT IMPLEMENTATION

According to our research, the composite best practices of implementing SBIRT in worldwide studies of which we are aware of include:

- Identify at least one office staff recovery champion in each practice
- Train office doctors, other prescribers, and office staff recovery champions in the details of each SBIRT step
- Establish relationships with only quality area referral providers, including peer recovery and community support groups
- Align SBIRT with normal office patient flow
- Have disease education materials available
- Use a simple prescreening tool to identify those who need a further screening questionnaire/instrument to complete
- Integrate SBIRT into the electronic health record systems and report composite patient process and progress data
- Tailor strategies to meet practice site needs and ease of use
- Provide ongoing monitoring, consultation, and feedback to the patient
- Periodically reexamine the implementation of the SBIRT to promote improvements in cost, quality, and the efficiency of the process

One major common error that has occurred in SBIRT implementations is that once patients indicate a drinking or using problem (either voluntarily or through screening instruments), too often some doctors move from that initial indication directly to attempting a referral.

Patient choice, not coercion, is important at this initial juncture to establish trust. This is the point to begin the awareness of a recovery path for the patient, gently describing their screening results, asking non-threatening questions, and, unless they have acute symptoms, ensuring the patient can absorb the information, which should include a presentation of several options available for them to choose. One thing we know for sure is that denial of the disorder is often strong at this point, and trying to quickly prescribe a single solution for it is often resisted.

Unless the patient shows the need for immediate emergency or acute withdrawal management assistance, or unless the patient requests or willingly accepts an immediate referral to assessment, there are several other feasible options available to the doctor that will begin a reluctant or initially non-admitting, unwilling patient's road to potential recovery.

Part science, part art is needed when a doctor introduces any chronic, progressive, potentially fatal disease to a patient. An alcohol or other substance use disorder is no different than informing a patient they may have Parkinson's, cancer, or heart disease. Each person has their own reaction process and time to adjust. A new fear can surface quickly or slowly.

The doctor partners with the patient where they are, rather than expecting an immediate positive response to their secret being outed. This creates a better opportunity to start the patient on the path to recovery.

Often without any screening, when doctors refer patients directly to an assessment and treatment facility, the failure to address significant trust, stigma, disease education, motivation, and other upfront issues fosters patient reluctance, ending in unsuccessful referrals.

Initial patient intervention can include such services as initial medical assisted treatment (MAT) for assistance with cravings and withdrawal symptoms, patient/family disease education, thirty-day abstinence attempts, trial referrals to peer or community support groups, and other techniques to get the patient moving toward self-motivated recovery.

Most individuals with active alcohol or other substance use disorders are in full or partial denial or practice minimizing and other defense mechanisms to hide their disease. These psychological defenses sidetrack recovery efforts, allowing them to ignore their specific drinking or using issues causing their negative consequences. It would be nice if patients with the disease would be more open to immediate referral to treatment, but most need their pump primed with trust, knowledge and understanding before agreeing to need or get help.

A skillful doctor or other prescribing professional artfully builds the case and negotiates the plea in most cases when the patient opens their response with "not guilty" to what they may consider the topic to be a shameful, silent, hidden suffering. Dealing with substance misuse often requires patience, compassion, and tolerance. It's like field goal attempts in basketball, 50 percent success over a season is much better than not making any attempts to score at all!

With proper administrative support, I say to you doctors, existing medical practices, and health care systems: You Can Do This! Think of the suffering, the costs and deaths you can prevent by earlier screening for the nation's number one direct and indirect death threat!

ENDNOTES

1. Gabor Maté, M.D., In the Realm of Hungry Ghosts: Close Encounters with Addiction, p. 3, North Atlantic Books, revised 2020
2. Jensen and Damon Winter, Help and Hope for People with Addiction, Interlandi, *New York Times*, December 17, 2023.
3. Ibid.
4. US Public Health Service, Facing Addiction in America, The Surgeon General's Report on Alcohol, Drugs and Health, Vivek Murphy, M.D., MBA, Vice Admiral p.–10, 2016
5. JAMA Network OPEN, Physician Reluctance to Intervene In Addiction, July 2024
6. Ibid., Maté, p.xvii, quote from Breaking Down the Walls by Alice Miller, North Atlantic Books, revised 2020
7. The Four Noble Truths of Buddhism and Upinshads Hinduism scriptures
8. Ibid., Maté, p. 305
9. Stalker, Rev. James, D.D, The Seven Deadly Sins and the Seven Cardinal Virtues, p.53, originally published by the American Tract Society, 1901,1902
10. Eckhart Tolle, The Power of Now, p.304, Namaste Publishing, 1999
11. Lembke, Dr. Anna, Dopamine Nation: Finding Balance in the Age of Indulgence, p.3, Penguin Random House, 2021
12. Ibid., Maté, p. 193
13. Ibid., Maté, p. 217
14. National Institute on Alcohol Abuse and Addiction, "Alcohol Screening and Brief Intervention for Youth: A Practitioner's Guide", NIH, 2011
15. Phillips, J.B., Your God is Too Small: A Guide for Believers and Skeptics Alike, Simon and Schuster, 2012
16. Humphrey, Keith, PhD, et.al., Alcoholics Anonymous: Most Effective Path to Alcohol Abstinence, a Study by The Stanford School of Medicine, 2020
17. Grisel, Dr. Judith, Never Enough: The Neuroscience and Experience of Addiction, p. 30, Doubleday, 2019
18. Ibid., Grisel, Dr. Judith, p. 93
19. "How It Works", The Big Book of Alcoholics Anonymous, p. 58, 2001 (Fourth Edition)
20. The Twelve Steps and Twelve Traditions of Alcoholics Anonymous, p. 48

21. James, William, <u>A Variety of Religious Experiences</u>, Lecture IX Conversion, Megalodon Entertainment, 2008 (Originally Published 1902)
22. Drinking Patterns, Alcohol Research, Current Reviews, p. 17–18 January 2018
23. Gollum, Trammell, Joint Study, University Iowa and University Copenhagen, Cell Metabolism, 2022
24. Dick, Dr. Danielle M., Agrawal, A., <u>The Genetics Of Alcohol And Other Drug Dependence</u>, Alcohol Research and Health (2), p. 111-119, 2008
25. Ibid., Dick, Agrawal
26. Kessler, David A., M.D., <u>Capture Point: Unraveling The Mystery of Mental Suffering</u>, p. 7-8, Harper Collins, 2016
27. Ibid.
28. Knapp, Caroline, <u>Drinking: A Love Story</u>, page 52-53, Dial Press Trade, 1997
29. Lembke, Anna, <u>Dopamine Nation: Finding Balance in the Age of Indulgence</u>, p. 63, Penguin Random House, 2021
30. Ibid., Lembke, p. 2
31. Ibid., Lembke, p. 49
32. Ibid., Kessler, p. 41
33. Ibid., Knapp, p. 53
34. Ibid., Lembke, p. 53
35. Ibid., Koob, p. 57
36. Duhigg, Charles, <u>The Power of Habit</u>, p. 19, Random House, 2014
37. Clear, James, <u>Atomic Habits: Tiny Changes, Remarkable Results,</u> Random House, 2018
38. Ibid., Duhigg, p. 25-26
39. Mooney, Al J., M.D., <u>The Recovery Book</u>, p. 202-203, Workman Publishing, 1992
40. Erickson, Carlton K., PhD, <u>The Disease of Pleasures: The Science of Addiction</u>, Norton Books
41. Haroutnian, Harry, M.D., <u>Being Sober</u>, p. 48, Rodale Books, 2013
42. Ibid., Maté, p. 116
43. Ibid., Haroutnian, p. 37
44. Ibid., Grisel, p. 182
45. Hari, Johann, <u>Lost Connections</u>, p.59, Bloomsbury Publishing, 2018
46. Ibid., Kessler, p. 14
47. Urshel, Harold C. III, MD, <u>Healing the Addicted Brain</u>, p. 13, SourceBooks, 2009
48. Ibid., Maté, p. 366
49. Thomas, Paul, M.D. and Jennifer Margulis, PhD., <u>The Addiction Spectrum</u>, p.67, Harper One, 2018
50. Ibid., Haroutunian, p. 7
51. Harrison, Thomas F. and Connery, Hilary S., M.D., PhD, <u>The Complete Family Guide to Addiction</u>, Chapter 8, The Guilford Press, 2019
52. Ibid., Grisel, p. 23
53. Ibid., Maté, p. 149
54. Ibib., Maté, p. 168

55. Ibid., Maté, p. 147
56. Ibid., Grisel, p. 13
57. Ibid., Grisel, p. 31
58. Ibid., Grisel, p. 34; quote of Minsky, Marvin, <u>Society of Mind</u>, Simon & Schuster, 1988
59. Solomon, Richard L. and Corbitt Joh,n D., "<u>An Opponent Process Theory of Motivation</u>", *Psychological Review*, page 81, 1974
60. Ibid., Koob, p. 22
61. Solof, Dr. Barry MD, FASAM, <u>Public Health Enemy Number One – The Therapist's Guild to Addictive Medicine</u>, p. xii-xv (Introduction) Central Recovery Press, 2013
62. Murthy, Dr. Vivek, <u>U.S. Surgeon General Calls for Cancer Warnings on Alcoholic Beverages</u>, The Wall Street Journal, 2025
63. Szalavitz, Maia, <u>Undoing Drugs: How Harm Reduction is Changing the Future of Drugs and Addiction</u>, p.7, Hachette Books, 2021
64. Barton, Antigone, <u>Florida Shuffle: State's Failure To Oversee Addiction Treatment Leaves Patients In Deadly Danger</u>, The Palm Beach Post, September 2023
65. Steven W., <u>Don't Quit Booze, Just Drink Differently</u>, The Guardian, 2024
66. Owens, Caitlin, The Addiction Crisis Is Even Worse Than Headlines Can Convey, Axios, May 2024
67. Lovett, Laura, Hazelden Betty Ford Foundation Reports Surge in Revenue Amid Rising Demand for Residential, Detox Services, Behavioral Health Business, August 2024
68. Parshall, Allison, Scientific American, August 19, 2024
69. Crews, Fulton T., Coleman, Jr., Leon G., Macht, Victoria A., Vetreno, Ryan P., Alcohol, HMGB1, and Innate Immune Signaling in the Brain, Alcohol Research: Current Reviews, August 2024

www.ingramcontent.com/pod-product-compliance
Lightning Source LLC
Chambersburg PA
CBHW040000080526
44586CB00027B/2827